About Earline

Other titles by
Carol Ann Wilson
Still Point of the Turning World:
The Life of Gia-fu Feng

About Earline

With Love & Best Wishes to Lucretia
Carol & Earline
2010.

Carol Ann Wilson

Boulder, Colorado

© 2011 Carol Ann Wilson

All rights reserved.

No portion of this book may be reproduced, distributed, or transmitted in any form or by any means, including photocopying, recording, or other electronic or mechanical methods, without the prior written permission of the publisher, except in the case of brief quotations embodied in critical reviews and certain other noncommercial uses permitted by copyright law. For permission requests, write to the author at the address below.

ISBN-13: 978-1460970157

www.carolannwilson.info

Cover and text design: suecampbellgraphicdesign.com
Cover photo: Earline Wilson

Excerpt from an article on the Wilson House, page 219, featured in the *Florence Citizen*, Florence Colorado, used with permission.

Printed in United States of America

this book is written
about and for
my mother

and has been penned
with gentleness and love

Prologue

Walter's resonant, expressive voice filled his children's ears and fired their imaginations as they sat clustered around him. He read with a flair that invited the young ones to lose themselves in one adventure after another, raising goose bumps, stoking dreams and fantasies. Reading Zane Grey, Vereen Bell, and others, his voice brought adventure to them, from the swamps of the south and across the wild west. It brought triumph—good over evil, bravery in the face of overwhelming challenge, discoveries of the pot of gold at rainbow's end. And it brought the finding of the way home, to a home that was loving, happy, full of joy.

Reading to them, and often their friends, from the *Saturday Evening Post*, Walter's voice transported them to worlds beyond the small parcel of land on which they lived and which they tilled, to excitement and daring far beyond their everyday lives. They basked in it, each week looked forward to it, and, as children do, saw their own lives potentially full of similar novelty and adventure. In them, particularly Earline, fourth child and first daughter, those stories planted seeds that took root and nurtured her already daring inclinations.

While Walter stoked the fires of adventure, their mother Mittie embodied patience and love, teaching by example. Earline observed her mama's kindness to strangers, those hoboes who knew the way to their house and marked it for others. For poor as they were, Mittie always had food for the hungry and less fortunate, and time for the sick or forsaken. She guided Earline up into her teens and strove to teach her headstrong girl patience.

Then in her late teens, Earline's restlessness and need to find some way to express herself pressed her to action, even though she didn't know what the consequences might be. In that time, as in so many others to come, she took a first step and then followed the course that opened up before her. Like a Florida "Alice" stepping though a pineywoods looking glass, Earline let her curiosity guide her. Propelled by need, whether physical or emotional, she took the option that most clearly presented itself and didn't worry over alternatives. And as in those stories her daddy read to them, she entrusted herself to adventure, to novelty, to finding where her idealized version of reality might finally play out and then, to seeking a way back to a happy home.

Chapter One

Postcard Days

She was bored. The sameness of the days stretched behind her like a late afternoon shadow. Sameness loomed before her like a dark cloud. She felt bored with being bored. Trapped, she was stuck in tiny Inwood, in the backwoods of Jackson County, a mostly rural, agricultural county in the Florida panhandle where she'd lived all nineteen of her years. With no means other than her own two feet to go the five miles to Sneads, with its booming population of one thousand, Earline couldn't even have a job, even if there'd been one. It was April, 1942. Spring, a time of renewal, growth, blossoms, and Earline found herself stagnating.

Two of her older brothers, J.W. and Melvin, had joined up when they heard about Pearl Harbor. They'd all been sitting there that Sunday in 1941, listening to the radio Earline had bought for five dollars, paying a dollar on it whenever she'd saved enough from her various jobs, before they'd moved to Inwood. Eventually, she'd paid the whole five dollars, and the radio became the family's lifeline to the world. Then came Pearl Harbor, and on that radio they listened as President Roosevelt spoke on December 8th, speaking of the "date that would live in infamy."

Glued to their respective spots and hanging on his every word, they listened as the President asked Congress to declare war.

Few young American men could ignore what this meant. No questions, no doubt, no waiting, J.W. and Melvin joined up, along with thousands of others. The next thing Earline knew they were off to prepare to fight. J.W. would end up in the 101st Airborne, eventually becoming a paratrooper and undertaking exceptionally dangerous missions with the Army's Screaming Eagles, often jumping behind enemy lines to relay critical information. Melvin would drive tanks and fight with General George Patton. But Earline didn't know, couldn't know, these details at the time. She only knew that two of her brothers and most of the other young men around there were off to the war. They had a mission, a purpose, albeit a highly dangerous one.

With Melvin and J.W. gone, Uncle Lon now in charge of the five younger siblings, and no job to be had, one boring day followed another for Earline. On one of these days, she went for a walk.

Breathing in the pleasing scent of honeysuckle, she ambled down the red clay road, heading toward Highway 90, which ran east and west across the panhandle and to the far side of the country. All around her birds sang—wood thrush, quail, and dove. Mockingbirds joined in, mimicking, and mocking. The sounds brought some comfort, the lively calls, announcements, pronouncements of the free, the unconfined.

Earline's love of nature held particularly strong with birds, flowers and trees. She appreciated the fresh greenness surrounding her, the burst of plant life, the promise it seemed to hold. But still she longed for adventure, the kind featured in the few movies she'd seen, in the books she'd managed to get her hands on. Not much adventure around these parts, which was why some of the young people she knew had wandered away, a few going as far as California.

Along the highway cars and pick-up trucks passed by, mostly old ones. Who could afford anything new? But even if money was scarce, friendliness wasn't. People waved as they passed and occasionally accompanied the wave with the "ahooga" of a Model A Ford.

Chapter One: Postcard Days

Earline was waving to a passing truck when she heard the woosh of tires on pavement behind. A black coupe pulled to a stop beside her and a man, woman and two kids peered through the windows. The woman, young and well groomed, leaned her head out and called to Earline, "Hey, you want a ride? We're going quite a ways and can drop you wherever you'd like."

Pausing only an instant, Earline smiled back at the friendly woman and said, "Why, yes. That would be nice."

She climbed into the back with the kids, sank into the seat's relative softness, and beamed at the young family. Her body tingled with anticipation for even this little adventure, for the novelty and freedom, however limited, it presented. Earline was not yet aware that this was her first step into a much bigger, longer adventure. She didn't realize that when the family came to the end of their journey somewhere farther west on Highway 90, it would be only the first part of hers.

Some sixty-eight years later, when asked about her decision to keep going, amused and perhaps a bit offended, she would say, "I didn't decide. I just did it." Given the opportunity, she entrusted herself to a journey into the unknown by taking that first unforeseen step. Why not take the next?

SHE STANDS IN THE SNOW, A PROFUSION OF EVERGREENS behind her—all ninety-seven pounds of her clad in the blue short-sleeved shirt and lighter blue slacks she was wearing when she went out for a walk, nearly a week earlier. Dark hair, almost collar length, frames a youthful face lit by her radiant smile. She exudes joy, confidence, and an eagerness for whatever is to come next. It's the only photograph of that trip, understandably a keeper, maybe one of the earliest photos of Earline. Her family had never been able to afford a camera, and it would be a while before Earline could buy her own.

The young priest who'd picked her up somewhere in Texas had a Kodak Brownie. The picture was taken at Lake Tahoe, and he made sure she eventually got a copy. Part-way through Texas on his way to San Francisco, he'd seen her by the highway and stopped to offer her a ride. She hesitated before accepting; she'd ridden only with families so far. But he explained that he was a priest, pointing to his collar as evidence. Although not quite sure what a priest was, Catholics being few and far between in Jackson County, she figured it was somehow related to a church, and she accepted. She rode all the way to California with him.

A kind man, he seemed to Earline more like an uncle than a preacher. Though she would long remember his clerical collar and his warm generosity, time would erase the memory of his name. Because he found Earline to be interested, he talked to her about engaging things—places he'd traveled, people he'd met. He openly delighted in Earline's awe of new sights, her sense of wonder at how big the country was, her glee even as they encountered new vistas, canyons, mountains, the desert, snow.

Especially Colorado. The mountains astonished her. A ways into Colorado she first saw them off in the distance, and she could hardly believe they were real. Though small because they were still far away, the long line of white-topped mountains rose from the horizon, beckoning. They lured her, caught her imagination.

Between the travelers and the mountains lay Denver, the big city an experience even in passing. Denver seemed to go on forever, and the traffic surpassed anything Earline had yet come upon. Eventually they reached the city's western boundaries and continued on U.S. Highway 6, entering Clear Creek Canyon. She could barely breathe, encountering seemingly endless walls of rock rising straight up, embracing the road on both sides. Clear Creek, more energetic than any body of water she'd ever seen, danced and shouted all the way down the canyon, greeting them at every turn in its rush downhill.

They emerged from the canyons, yet felt the foothills still holding them close, sturdily reminding her of her relative unimportance. And then majesty appeared up close in the huge, towering, snow-covered peaks, the ones that forever after she would love, long for, dream about. For this was true love—this part of Earth that wedged itself in her heart. She knew she would return, stay here for some important part of her life. When that would be, or how, she didn't know, but she knew it lay ahead in her life.

More new sights, long to be remembered, etched themselves into her young, impressionable mind. The desert for one, vast, dry, and emptier than anyplace she could've imagined, having spent her life in the semi-tropics enclosed in multiple shades of green. Early one morning, somewhere in that great expanse of desert, the priest stopped for a rest break. They both needed to stretch their legs after so many hours in the car. Lighting a cigarette, one of the few he'd smoked along the way, he inhaled deeply, exhaled slowly, blowing the smoke upwards. The fragrance of spicy tobacco drifted through the crisp, clean air, air already redolent with the scent of sage and spring wildflowers. Earline thought it one of the most wonderful smells ever. She never forgot it.

They motored on through Salt Lake City, where she saw the Mormon Tabernacle as they traveled along the wide, orderly streets. They stopped so the priest could buy Earline a pair of shorts to wear with a shirt he loaned her. He said she'd probably like to go for a swim. And she did, after marveling at the astounding sight now before her, her biggest thrill, the Great Salt Lake. The thirty-seventh largest lake in the world. The fourth largest terminal lake, one with no outlet other than evaporation, although Earline didn't yet know these facts. Her amazement at its size almost equaled her surprise at the ease with which she could float in it. She always did float easily and naturally, but this water carried floating to a whole new level.

"Why is the water salty? How can you float like that? How big is this lake? Is it really a lake? Does it get very deep in the middle? How does it stay this big?"

Asking a million questions, she wanted to explore everything she possibly could in and around that giant, shallow body of water. The priest indulged her curiosity as much as he could, and then it was time to move on, for they both understood she could never know enough. But for Earline, this was what life was meant to be—discovery, novelty, adventure, continuous stimulation. She couldn't ever have enough. And like the two-sided coin, the double-edged sword, she would find throughout her life that such a hunger could bring delight when fed, and misery when denied.

The stop by Lake Tahoe provided another brief respite before the final push to San Francisco. The snow, the lake, the mountains brought more amazement, more wonder. Would it never end? She hoped not—for more than one reason.

First came the sheer joy of discovery, of seeing the beauty, and even the drabness, of the world beyond Inwood. So much variety. So much everything. It took her beyond herself, beyond her life of limited possibilities—beyond those suffocating constraints. Now free, now flying as she'd never flown before, she wished the adventure to go on and on.

This desire led to the second reason, so intertwined with the first that she could hardly recognize it—these novel experiences sometimes crowded out the sadness she'd experienced in her young life. That sad feeling crept in still, sometimes when she was tired, sometimes when conversation with the priest lagged and mile after silent mile lulled her defenses. At home she'd tried to find work to help out the family, and she had found a few temporary jobs. But after those few opportunities, the only plentiful things were empty days and nights. She pushed those feelings away, for that's how she'd learned to cope, and it was a coping mechanism she would rely on far beyond her young years.

Again she watched the passing scenery and tried thinking about something else, something that made her feel better. The kids. Her younger brothers and sisters. How she wished they could see all this! Their dear images crowded her mind: Betty, age sixteen, whose blonde hair gradually was turning dark; also blond Jack at fourteen;

Chapter One: Postcard Days

whose hair would stay that way; darker Linwood, twelve; chestnut-brown Jimmy, eight; and redheaded Rubye, now four and a half.

But worry crept in underneath. The niggling, worrying thoughts could grow out of hand in a hurry. Were the kids okay? Were her oldest brother Red and his wife Margaret able to help Uncle Lon enough? In Inwood Red and Margaret lived with them in that old house that used to be a school. Having them there made the house's three big rooms a little more crowded, but Margaret could look after the kids during the day while Uncle Lon was doing the little farming he could. The logging had stopped when her daddy got sick, and Uncle Lon did his best trying to farm, just as he did his best with the kids. Red would be off working in Chattahoochee, about eight miles away. The arrangement gave Red and Margaret an affordable place to start their married life while helping hold family together.

She hoped they'd gotten her postcard, telling them not to worry about her. She was fine, she was safe. People were kind, giving her rides, looking out for her. But she didn't know about them, about how they were now.

≫•≪

SAN FRANCISCO. MORE PEOPLE BUNCHED TOGETHER THAN she'd imagined in all of California. Tall, skinny houses, office buildings, restaurants, dry-goods shops, laundries and markets marched up and down the steep hills and also settled in between. Buses, streetcars, paneled delivery trucks, new sedans, Model Ts, and Model As crowded the streets. Horns honked, trolley bells clanged, the buzz of activity electrified the air. Sharp smells, sweet smells, pungent smells filled her nose. Tall, short, fat, thin, brown, white, black—all kinds of people she'd never seen and some she had crowded the sidewalks and shops. Silk dresses, hats with veils, fancy suits, sailor uniforms, doorman uniforms, police uniforms, butcher aprons, beggars' rags. Her mind boggled.

The priest negotiated the city's maze with no little skill. He knew of a small efficiency apartment where she could stay for a few days, another bit of good fortune for Earline.

Time has blurred some details but can never dull Earline's memory of her first Chinese meal, and this in Chinatown. She will ever after declare it the best meal she's ever eaten. There were platters overflowing with shrimp and chicken in exotic sauces, rice fried with unknown vegetables, noodles in fragrant brown liquid, crispy egg rolls, flowery-scented tea. All was placed before her, all within her reach, and that southern girl was in food heaven.

Another time they ate at an Italian restaurant, yet another opportunity for Earline to learn about different food. Looking at the menu, she asked, "What are a-n-c-h-o-v-i-e-s?" not daring to pronounce the unfamiliar word.

Grinning, the priest pronounced it for her. "Little fish, sometimes used for bait, but also preserved in salt and oil for humans." Then he laughed, seeing the visceral reaction on Earline's face.

"I don't think I can eat those."

"Yes, you can. They're safe. It's alright to eat them."

She ended up taking a small bite from his order, but that so-called delicacy would never count among Earline's favorites.

The priest had to attend to his work, so Earline explored San Francisco on her own for a short while. She soon decided that less time in the city would be better. Coming from her quiet country corner of Florida that consisted of a dirt road and a few houses, to this enormous, chaotic place confused her. So, with her yearning for continuous movement and new sights, especially those of nature, now in her blood, she looked for the best way out of town. She'd let the priest know she was leaving. He wanted her to write, to keep in touch; she wanted to stay in contact with this new friend and promised she would.

Expecting rides still to come as easily as they had so far, she didn't worry about getting them or about the people who would stop for her. She wasn't afraid at all because in her experience she found that people were just plain nice. For the past decade, with

Chapter One: Postcard Days

the whole country hard hit by the Great Depression and its recovery achingly slow, people looked after others, as her mama fed those hoboes. Maybe now it was because the country was involved in a major war and, given the common threat, people just naturally drew closer together, trying to help each other. The war would bring better economic times, but in the spring of 1942, that wasn't evident yet. But whatever the combination of circumstances, Earline found many folks were just like that wonderful priest.

Some of the care and concern people showed could have been due to how young she looked, younger even than her nineteen years. Being very pretty didn't hurt, either, nor did her gratitude, her sincere appreciation for every kindness. Since she didn't have money, people often gave her some, as well as something to eat. It seemed most wanted to share what they had—rides, food, companionship and yes, even money. And Earline was always thankful.

Once in the early part of the trip, somewhere in Alabama, someone had asked where she was going. Not expecting the question, not knowing herself where she was headed, and definitely not wanting the nice person to worry, she came up with something to reassure, to put a mind at ease. It surprised even her when the words came out of her mouth. "To California, to see my aunt."

Asked at what address, Earline shrugged. "I don't know. She told me to look in the phone book and find it." Inventive, some might say.

Now in California and the imaginary aunt only a faint memory, Earline continued her travels with greater confidence. Looking for a way out of the city, she wandered down a street where she saw several women standing together. The way they were standing and talking to each other perplexed Earline. All dressed up and looking really nice in their softly colored silk skirts and tops and their high-heeled shoes, several leaned against the slightly shabby building, all were laughing. They seemed friendly enough to approach. Typically curious and still inexperienced enough to be candid, she asked what they were doing.

One of the women, who looked kind, smiled at Earline. "Well, you're just a little bit young to know about that."

More puzzled, Earline looked at the other three women. They, too, smiled at her but offered no information. Still curious but sensing the women weren't going to tell her much, she decided to ask only for the directions she needed—which highway to take out of San Francisco.

"Which way are you going?"

What a question. Earline hadn't even thought about direction, only of getting out of the city and not of what might be next. "North," she said. After all, she was from the South and she sure didn't want to go back in that direction yet.

Pointing down the street, one woman said, "Take a left at the intersection. That street will lead you toward the highway."

But before she could leave, the women began asking questions of their own.

"Where are you from, honey?"

"What brings you here?"

"Where're you really headed?"

And finally, "How do you keep so clean traveling like this," the questioner pointing at her tiny suitcase. The fact was she didn't need a big one since she still had little more than the clothes she was wearing the day she left home.

"I wash my clothes every night and dry them as much as I can. I squeeze them in a towel then hang them up to dry. Then I put my slacks under the mattress in the morning to press them."

Memories of the many damp mattress bottoms she'd left behind floated through her mind along with the hope that none of them had mildewed. She also thought of the nights she hadn't had a bed, as when she'd slept in a car traveling through the night. But her desire to stay clean combined with her resourcefulness fairly ensured she would find some way to bathe regularly and do her laundry.

As she started down the street, the women wished her well and even gave her a little money for food. It wasn't until later that she

Chapter One: Postcard Days

remembered the odd word one of the women used when she whispered to another, "She doesn't know about a crib." And it was even later that she learned its meaning.

Bolstered by the directions and some vague sense of where she was going, she found her way out of San Francisco and with only a short wait caught a ride going north. New sights beckoned. The road north called and Earline accepted its invitation.

THESE WERE POSTCARD DAYS, AND FOR EARLINE IMPRESSIONS from them would remain with her always. The beautiful, awe-inspiring sights, the freedom of letting life unfold, letting the adventures come, trusting that food and rides would appear, that all would be okay. And given all that she'd lost in recent years, along with the utter boredom and sense of uselessness she'd felt in Inwood, escaping into a postcard seemed a pretty good thing to do.

Decades later, recounting her adventures, Earline won't remember all the details of who gave her rides, who provided food, cash. But she will remember that only once did she fear she would go hungry. Recounting that time, she began with what became a familiar refrain, a theme of her travels. "Oh, everybody gave me money. Those were hard times and people shared. I never was really hungry, but I sure got scared I was going to get hungry one time." That it was only one time was something.

She was somewhere near Portland, Oregon, and had just mailed home some silver dollars, a coin for each brother. She'd saved every penny she could from the money people had given her, then traded the coins for the big silver ones. She wouldn't know until much later that those coins never made it to the boys, and she could only guess at what could've happened to them.

Walking over a railroad trestle, she heard voices yelling at her. She looked down to see some older teenagers swimming in the river below. They invited her to join them, and she couldn't resist. She changed into her shorts and a shirt behind a tree and jumped into the cool, refreshing water. Being with young people, laughing, playing in the water restored her. And then she was on her way again.

Tired and with only fifteen cents in her pocket, nevertheless she wanted to stay on the move. On the outskirts of Eugene, a trucker stopped, the only trucker she rode with.

She recalled his thoughtfulness. "You look worn out. You want to sleep behind the seat? I'm gonna stop in a while for something to eat, but you can crawl back there and rest for a bit."

Appreciating the opportunity to rest, she did crawl behind the seat to the tiny sleeping area there. Big enough for one person, it easily accommodated her tiny figure. Although sleep evaded her, she was relieved to just to lie down, to rest knowing she was still on the road.

An hour or so later, they stopped at a restaurant, and there their paths diverged. Earline used her fifteen cents to buy a hamburger and a coke, which satisfied her teen-age hunger, while the trucker ate more heartily and drank strong, hot coffee. Earline thanked him as they parted, the trucker heading farther north. Earline had decided to head east, toward Montana. She was following her nose, following her curiosity about the west.

As had happened so often, just as one good thing ended, another presented itself. Sort of like rabbits being pulled out of a hat, she described it in later years. You couldn't possibly think things would keep happening this way, but they did. The young waitress who took Earline's order at the truck stop asked her where she was going.

"I'm traveling to see all of the West I can see. I want to know what's out here."

"Do you have any money?"

"No. That fifteen cents was it."

"Well, there's a motel out there. Here's a dollar. Go get some rest!"

Grateful again, Earline accepted the dollar and got a room for seventy-five cents. She bathed, washed the clothes she was wearing, hung them up to dry, and fell asleep as soon as her head hit a most welcomed pillow.

Chapter One: Postcard Days

She slept a deep dreamless sleep, unfettered by fear or worry, a sleep reflecting nineteen years of uncomplicated, sheltered life. Sheltered, for despite her adventuresome nature, despite her impulsiveness, despite loss, she had yet to experience cruelty, viciousness or evil. Some might call that girl naive, vulnerable, and in some ways they would be right. But these qualities seemed to inspire a protectiveness, a generosity in others. At least, so far they had. But her luck was soon to change.

Now in central Oregon, for the third time in several thousand miles of travel, a lone man stopped to give her a lift. Her experiences with the priest and the trucker had been so good, she hesitated only a moment before accepting and climbing into the two-door coupe. But Earline's suspicions began to rise when, after only a few miles on the highway, the man turned off onto a dirt logging road. He drove up the road, past several parked logging trucks, heading farther back into the forest. Finally, he parked the car and turned toward her, his arm snaking over to rest on her shoulders.

Terrified, yet quick-thinking and resolute to stop any further advances, Earline looked at him and smiled sweetly. "Why don't you come around to this door?" she suggested, employing her southern drawl for all it was worth and gesturing toward the door with her right hand.

The man jumped out of the car and, slamming the door shut, hurried around to Earline's side. But he didn't hurry fast enough to prevent Earline from leaning slightly to pick up one of the several Coke bottles lying in the car's litter at her feet. Eagerly he grabbed the handle, opened her door, and inclined his body toward her.

She sprang at him like a cat, whacking him on the head with a force belying her small frame. Down he went, hitting the ground with a sickening thud. Earline grabbed her little suitcase, jumped from the car, and streaked down the road, her heart pounding so hard she thought it would explode. As she rounded a curve, she saw a logging truck coming up the road. The driver saw her, saw how frantic and disheveled and she looked, and stopped.

"Is there trouble?" he asked.

"Yes, there's a man back there. I hit him with a Coke bottle, and he needs . . . I hope I didn't kill him or anything."

"Do you want a ride out? I'll take you wherever you want to go, to the road, or somewhere safe."

Earline scrambled up and into the passenger side. As the truck lumbered down to the highway, Earline filled him in on what had happened. She asked him to drive on the highway a little ways in the same direction from which she'd come, figuring that when the man came out of the woods, he'd go the other way. Or at least she hoped so.

The logger drove a few miles up the highway. Earline asked him if he'd check on the possibly still-unconscious man, and he said he would. He wasn't happy about leaving her at the side of the road, but she insisted, and he agreed. She thanked him for his kindness, his help, and watched him turn the long truck around at a turnout and drive back down the highway. She hoped the other man wasn't dead, but she also hoped she'd never see him again.

When, after only a short wait, a family stopped to offer her a ride, she accepted with relief. Eager to be away from the only trouble she'd encountered on this whole trip, she knew that trouble had made her a little less naive, a little less trusting, and probably a little more safe.

Chapter Two

Every Child's Fantasy

One way to cope with life's troubling events is to keep moving, a response that would thread itself throughout much of Earline's life. Sometimes movement would lead to better things, other times it would be only a temporary way to avoid an undesirable situation. But after escaping her Oregon attacker, her inclination to move on took her far from the unnerving incident, which marked a dramatic and troubling end to those lovely postcard days, to something else wonderful—living every child's fantasy. It happened on the 4th of July in Red Lodge, Montana, where she came across several carnivals joined together for a big celebration.

As she reveled in every sight, sound, and scent, Earline breathed in the smell of roasting peanuts, popcorn, cotton candy; stepped into the sounds of music from merry-go-rounds, people shouting, laughing. She marveled at big tents packed with side-shows—a magician, swordbox, flame swallower, and more. And then she spied a real-life, loop-de-loop airplane ride.

The plane's astounding stunts captured her complete attention. She watched, her mouth open. Next to her stood a big, blond man with a lilting accent, whom she'll remember only as the "big Swede." He turned to look down at her and asked, "Do you want to take the ride?"

"Of course, I do!" She meant it with every molecule of her being, but she couldn't, wouldn't, say that she wanted that ride more than just about anything she'd ever wanted in her life. So close to doing something most people only dream of, thinking about it made her insides quiver. But in case she didn't get it, she wasn't about to show how much she wanted it. Only that she did.

He bought tickets for both of them, and they stood in line awaiting their turn. Before long, they were next. The open cock-pit plane held only two people besides the pilot. Looking around as she climbed up the few steps to the plane, Earline could see there wasn't much to it. No cover over their heads. Only the two seats and their straps in that metal shell. Just the basics. Earline and the big Swede crawled onto their seats, side-by-side behind the pilot, strapped themselves in, and prepared for the ride of their lives.

She heard the engine revving, felt the plane moving, then bumping along, taxiing to gain speed. Earline bounced with each bump, looking straight ahead and swallowing hard. Small as she was, she could see only the leather cap covering the back of the pilot's head. She felt the bumpiness melt away as the plane's wheels left solid ground. Turning to look back, then down at the crowd, she watched the people below become smaller and smaller, then disappear altogether. Not because they were no longer there, not because the plane had gone so high, but because the plane had turned upside-down. She looked down, or up, at the sky. Her hair fell up, or was that down? Suspended in air, in time, Earline could only take in momentary impressions as her stomach lurched up to her throat and back with the pulling sensations of the plane's unexpected motion.

Then the plane rolled and she spied the crowd again. Just as quickly, it disappeared again. Then reappeared. Over and over, like a peek-a-boo game, the tiny figures below appeared, disappeared, reappeared. A shivering mass by now, her stomach threatened to rebel, an uprising that took much of her will to quiet.

But this wasn't all. Just when she was beginning to adjust to rolling sideways over and over, the plane moved forward, nose up, pushing the two passengers back in their seats. They seemed to be going straight up into the heavens. But no, they were on their heads again, up-side-down, doing a real-life, toe curling, heart-stopping loop-de-loop.

Time suspended itself. Her heart stopped. Her breathing stopped. Then, she felt the airplane's tires touch the ground, with only a slight jolt, and they taxied to a stop. Stunned, unbelieving, feeling like corn in that popper on the midway finally coming to rest, she turned unseeing eyes toward the crowd. Had she really done what she thought she'd just done? Had she really flown, turned cartwheels in the sky? Life could never be the same.

Several men ran up to the plane. Earline watched as they helped the Swede unfasten his safety belt and supported him as he slowly, shakily, slid down to the ground. His face seemed even more pale than before, his breathing uneven. His knees were so weak, he couldn't walk without help; the men on each side of him half-carried him away from the plane.

When it was Earline's turn, she'd already unfastened her safety belt, ready. A couple of men reached out to help her, but she waved them away. "I can get out by myself," forcing her southern drawl to come out even and calm.

Unaided by anyone or anything other than her determination not to show fear or any slight hint of it, she stepped out and steadily, she hoped again, walked away from the plane.

Despite the lingering effects of the loop-de-loop plane ride—wobbly legs, queasy stomach, and scrambled brains—Earline marveled that she had actually been in that plane, knowing she'd left the earth's safety, gone up in an aeroplane and turned somersaults, flips, and twirls. She held the excitement close, wanted more, but she also wanted to get her feet back on the ground first. She'd always been awed by airplanes and their mystery, and now she'd been up in one.

Almost seven decades later she admitted, "Of course, I was afraid! But there was no way I was going to let anybody know that!" Her first airplane ride, and classic Earline, it was a doozy. It would be many years before she'd find herself in a plane again. But then some time during the 1970s, again in quintessential Earline fashion, she would take a few flying lessons.

She paused by the animal cages to gather herself. An elephant stood nearby, the chain around his huge leg attached to a stake close by. Right next to the elephant a cage held a couple of lions, one lying on his side asleep, the other lazily watching the people watching it. Earline had never seen such big animals, but the elephant looked bored, and she couldn't believe that sleeping creature in the cage could be king of the jungle. But after watching them only a few minutes, their inaction stirred her to action. She'd try to see them when they were performing.

She moved along to where a crowd had gathered, everyone's neck craned upwards. Earline looked up, too. And there were the Flying Ericksons, a high-wire and trapeze act, another first. Movies and stories didn't lie. It really did exist. Earline felt the line between real life and make-believe blur a little more.

Two young men and a young woman, wearing brilliant sequined, silk outfits, climbed high and then higher, up a soaring tower. Reaching the top, before Earline could blink, one of the men grabbed a trapeze and launched himself out into space, swinging in long arcs, back and forth, back and forth, smooth and relaxed as a swallow floating through the air at dusk. He kicked his legs out, gaining momentum, and swung back toward the platform. Pulling his legs over the trapeze bar and hanging from his knees as he glided through the air, he stretched his arms toward the young woman. She stepped off the tower, barely catching his hands. Earline gasped. The crowd gasped with her. She thought her neck would break, looking that far up. She held her breath as the woman dangled from the man's hands, twirling by one hand, spinning around and around. Then the woman swung back, flipped, and grasped a second trapeze just in time.

In the next instant the other man joined the woman on the

Chapter Two: Every Child's Fantasy

trapeze. He tossed her to the second man. Then that man tossed her back. Back and forth—several times. Finally, just when Earline thought she would pass out from tension, the young woman landed back on the tower platform, the two men right after her. They bowed to a screaming, cheering, applauding audience and climbed down to stand again on the safe, solid ground.

Earline, breathing again, wandered off to the see whatever came next. It didn't occur to her that, in a way, she had done exactly what that flying woman had done. She'd stepped off her home platform and made that first move out into the unknown. Those people who'd given her rides, money, and food were like those men in the act, keeping that woman moving through the air. And so far she'd landed feet-first, unharmed.

Watching the sword box act come to an end, Earline was surprised when a man dressed in a suit, vest, and top hat approached her. She wasn't aware that this man, Jimmy Queen, the owner's son, had been watching when she went up in that plane, and when she refused help getting out. She later found out he'd seen her wandering through the crowds and noticed that she wasn't with anyone. The two chatted for a few minutes as the crowd moved off, and then Jimmy asked, "You want a job?"

"What kind of job?"

"How about working the sword box here?" He grabbed her hand and took her over to the box to demonstrate how the girl got in and what she did.

Success in the sword box called for someone thin and flexible, someone who could bend around in a particular pattern to avoid being pierced by the swords. Traveling with the carnival required a spirit of adventure and no immediate ties. What could be a better fit? Earline signed on. Not only did it suit her at this time in her life, but some of the key things she would learn with the carnival and in the show business would serve her far into the future.

Officially a part of the Frank Burke Show, advertised as *The*

Cleanest Little Show on Earth, Earline continued her travels, now through Montana, Utah, Wyoming, and Colorado. In the company of good-hearted, interesting people, with the carnival's thrills and excitement and a paycheck to boot, throughout the summer months she truly was living every young person's dream.

Earline knew that traveling carnivals were popular entertainment during those times. Even the big posters stuck on buildings and store windows to advertise the show could draw small crowds. And during show time she could see for herself the delight and satisfaction the carnival brought to lives that consisted of too much hard work and not enough pay. The excitement she'd had so far had her hooked—the bustle and chaos of the midway with its freak shows, thrill acts, games of all sorts—shooting games, bottle games, skill games. The carousel, and of course carnival food—cotton candy, candied apples, ice cream, pop corn, and fried dough—seduced her along with carnival goers of all ages. Earline loved seeing the families there together, the mix of little kids, grandmas, young couples flirting with each other, even as hard times raged on. What she couldn't know was that, while some parts of the country were beginning to recover from the Great Depression and the recessions that followed, full recovery was still a few years away.

But Earline now had a job. In addition to working the sword box, bending and twisting into the tortuous positions required of her, she'd been offered a chance to be part of the Flying Ericksons' trapeze act, the show that usually topped off the evening. Earline wanted to do this, but she'd had no training, and that act required special skill. Reluctantly, she declined that offer.

She could, however, easily be the third and fourth legs for the four-legged woman. Marie, one of the Queen family, provided the first and second, along with the body. Full-length black stockings masked their different complexions, Marie's light and freckled, Earline's a little darker, without the freckles. Marie sat in full view, with Earline's legs protruding through two holes so that it really looked as if all four legs were Marie's. The rest of Earline was concealed behind the curtains, where she reclined against a bolster, also hiding the crowd from her. To illustrate Marie's authenticity, people were allowed to pinch the various legs. But the hapless or ill-intentioned onlooker who pinched too hard got a vicious kick from the often surprised, offended leg.

And then there was the electric chair, where she performed daily in rotation after the sword-box and four-legged woman acts. Billed as *Electra*, young, pretty Earline sat in the chair on a copper plate, demurely conducting a low-voltage charge while Jimmy Queen revved up the crowd.

"You gentlemen out there in the crowd had better be glad your wife doesn't have a stinger like this one!" And with those words, he touched a gasoline torch to Earline's tongue. The crowd would give a collective gasp as the torch burst into flames. To demonstrate Earline's other combustible abilities, he ignited a torch from her knee and then from her toe.

The time Jimmy slipped a nail onto the seat of the chair, Earline, unaware, sat down to begin the act. When her body made contact with the nail, the charge knocked her halfway across the tent. Furious, indignant, and spitting fire, Earline, Electra, gave old Jimmy quite a talking to, stinging him for all she was worth. That would be the last time he pulled such a stunt on her, but not the last time she'd let somebody know they were out of line. Earline did not then, nor ever, hold back when she felt wronged.

Working these three acts, Earline made five dollars a week, enough to cover her expenses, but just barely. Because there was no place for her to stay, she didn't sleep on the carnival grounds but always rented a room in town, usually at seventy-five cents a night, as did some of the others. Every day the carnival served the crew and performers pancakes, but there was a charge. A young man who befriended her, Joe Beale, a friend of the carnival owner, was along for the summer and worked with the machinery. He took it upon himself to look out for Earline, sometimes buying her food. She thought he followed her everywhere, believing he wanted to make sure she was safe. Another length in the thread running through this trip, people wanting to protect Earline seems a bit of irony, considering the way she dealt with that man back in Oregon. But everyone can benefit from friends who have their welfare in mind, and Earline was no exception.

After their acts, Earline and Marie Queen took advantage of the carnival's bounty, riding the Ferris wheel, tilt-a-wheel, merry-go-round and other rides. They'd get a special thrill when the big Ferris wheel stopped while they were on top and they could view the twinkling lights and bustling scene from the crown of their carnival world.

≫•≪

When the carnival finished its stint in a town, the grounds became a beehive of activity. Men swarmed everywhere, breaking down tents, folding and storing them in large containers, packing up equipment—sword box, electric chair, trapezes, food stalls. All of the equipment was then shipped by train and truck to the next town.

Between shows Earline traveled with a young Englishman and his wife, and often she went along with them to nightclubs in the evenings after the carnival closed for the day. Playing the horsehair fiddle and other homemade instruments, he'd sweep the audience away, and Earline with them, to enchanting places.

As that thin, young man sat on the stage playing lively tunes on his fiddle, Earline tapped toes and clapped hands along with the crowd. Growing quiet when he produced a melancholy ballad, they'd fall under his spell, some swaying slightly with the melodies. Sometimes he'd look up and grin at the audience, pushing his wispy, blond hair back from his eyes, and Earline could just see that bond between him and them tighten as if it were the strongest and most tender thing on earth. Her own fondness for him would swell at these moments, as the kind of pride she'd feel for an older brother flowed through her. He was, after all, a part of her carnival family.

Earline helped collect the coins that rained down on the stage, thrown by his now adoring fans. After the show, he'd always give her a portion of the offerings.

It seemed to Earline *The Cleanest Little Show on Earth* traveled everywhere. So much beauty, so many memorable sights. She tried to take in every detail to keep forever, not knowing that this trip would make an important geographical blueprint for her life, that decades later she would travel through many of these same places, both for the fun of it and also to earn a living.

One thing she'd always remember was that inspiring sight in the massive Big Horn Mountains in Wyoming. It happened in those magical moments when daylight seems to think about retreating, evening hovering around the edge. The Englishman, his wife, and Earline watched as a golden eagle flew in front of the car, his wingspread covering the road. Brown and golden feathers gleaming in the last rays of the sun, the bird swooped down, forcing them to slow the car to avoid hitting it. The eagle's appearance in those rugged, dramatic mountains, on that steep, curving road, and in the softly fading light seemed a special gift to the travelers.

Earline will also long remember the northeastern part of Colorado, when they played in Greeley. That community on the edge of the plains seemed so different from the spectacular landscape along U.S. Highways 6 and 40. Although no one could have known it, Greeley, where the Rocky Mountains reigned from a distance, was to be the last stop of the season. A train accident carrying the carnival's equipment to the next stop damaged the equipment sufficiently to send the Frank Burke show home early. It would head to St. Joseph, Missouri, to repair equipment and winter over until spring, when the carnival would blossom once again.

For Earline, those three months with new sights, new possibilities opening up almost daily had served as a balm to her sorrowful soul and inspiration to the free spirit in her. But it was time to go home. She missed her brothers and sisters and Uncle Lon. She wanted to see their faces, hear their voices, hug them, know for sure they were doing all right.

What she didn't yet realize was that the genie was out of the bottle, and she would never again be satisfied without the stimulation that came from meeting new people and seeing new places. This would be a theme, or perhaps a thorn, for her. Would she settle down and find contentment, or would she forever seek the excitement and adventure reflected in her postcard days and in the reality of the fantasy of carnival life she'd already lived?

CHAPTER THREE

Back to Memories

SOMETHING CHANGES INSIDE WHEN A YOUNG WOMAN'S restlessness has been met by discovery and challenge, by novel experiences and newly discovered friends. Yet the need to be with family and in familiar places has its draw, too. Somewhere deep inside, Earline knew the restlessness would come back, but she also knew she needed to touch down after so much had happened to her. It was kind of like that loop-de-loop plane ride. Loop-de-loop excitement was what she wanted from life, but she also needed time to take it all in, to come to a rest—at least temporarily, let everything that had happened settle in. Sort of like refueling to go up again. She didn't think much beyond that. Besides, after the carnival had had to close early, she couldn't see that she had much of a choice. She would return to the familiar and to those she loved, and she wouldn't dwell on the inevitable routine and sameness to come.

Like a boomerang, Earline was back. Back to her five younger siblings and Uncle Lon, all of whom she loved, all of whom provided the draw back to Florida. But now, despite that powerful draw, Inwood, Sneads, and Jackson County were even less appealing. Possibilities that had been only imagined before, now had living shape and form, they had the texture of varied landscapes, the thrill of crowds applauding, the anticipation of what each new day could bring. Changed, deepened, broadened as she was, such possibilities drew her even more.

But she loved her family, and so many cherished memories, both happy and heart-breaking, lived on here. Out West where each day brought something new, she'd had an easier time with those memories. But now here in the familiar South, too many of them came unbeckoned, too vivid.

Back only a few days and feeling the need for movement, she walked down the long clay road, images from childhood riding on the fresh early morning air, scenes from her very young days awakening with the bird song. She remembered rising with her mama at 4:00 in the morning to start the day's work. She'd been so little then, when her mama first taught her to make biscuits; she saw her small self on that orange crate, eager to learn and help. There were the tea parties Mittie devised, pouring milk for tea, teaching her daughter what a tea party was, with the beloved tea set Mittie'd somehow managed to get for her. Earline pictured the china doll Mittie ordered for her fourth birthday. When there was hardly ever money to spend on anything other than bare essentials, here came that undreamed-of gift. They'd been sitting at their orange crate tea table, she and her mama, when the mail carrier brought it. He'd handed the package to Mittie, and Earline remembered well the rare signs of excitement in her mama's shaking hands, the light in her brown eyes.

"Sister, wait till you see this!" her mama had said.

Pulling off the brown paper and opening the box, Earline first heard, then saw the gasp. Inside the box was the lovely doll and its broken head. Disappointment seeped into her, too, but she couldn't quite understand why her mama was crying. At four, she didn't know what it meant for her mother to plan and save for such a surprise, for something so beautiful for her little girl. For something so nearly out of reach. But in the years since, the weight of Mittie's disappointment and sadness over the broken doll had settled in, making Earline sad for them both.

She couldn't, wouldn't let herself think about those memories too long. They brought back that deep sadness, and her loneliness.

But sometimes annoying memories would save her from the too tender ones. How her brother J.W., three years older, loved to torment her. Having three older brothers wasn't always easy, and J.W. could be the most aggravating of the lot. He loved to put worms, cockroaches, anything crawly and creepy, down her back. She'd scream at him as she jumped around, wiggled, doing anything to make the thing drop out, creating just the reaction he'd hoped for. At some point, she'd caught on and began to tamp down her responses. Except when he went too far.

Once, in her early teens, J.W. smeared smelly, yellow chicken poop on her. Seeing that foul stuff streaked down her arm and leg sent her over the edge. She grabbed a metal rod that lay nearby and, with all the force of her fury, whammed J.W. It nearly broke his leg, but it stopped his shenanigans for a while. Later in life, Earline would attribute some of her toughness to having had six brothers, especially the three older ones, and especially J.W.

As for her two sisters, they came later. How vividly she remembered her third birthday, November 14, 1925. Sleeping on a pallet on the floor, she awoke when her mama came in holding a bundle in her arms. Even in the dim light Earline could see her mama's lovely, decidedly Cherokee features framed by her gleaming long, dark hair. Mittie knelt down and placed the bundle beside Earline, speaking softly, soothingly. "This is your sister. You must take care of her. She's your birthday present." A sister had come into Earline's life, Betty, the fifth child of what would eventually be nine—six boys and three girls.

The eldest, Edward, who would forever be known as Red, was born in 1915. Then, spaced about three years apart, came Melvin, John Walter (J.W.), Earline, and Betty. Jack, Linwood, Jimmy, and Rubye followed, also with about three-year spaces between them. Red and Rubye, bookends, both with their luminous red hair, were distinctive in the mix of the six dark-haired siblings and blond Jack.

The Scotch-Irish overrode the Cherokee in just the three. Five of them, including Earline had blue, blue eyes. The others looked out at the world through varying shades of brown and hazel, all except for Betty, who had one blue and one brown. Earline thought that just like Betty, if she couldn't decide, she'd take both colors.

Linwood, six years younger than Earline, was a smaller image of their daddy. Earline used to carry Lin around perched on her hip, although her mama told her to stop because it would make her hip lower on that side. Turned out it did cause some problems later on, but Earline loved carrying and watching after him. She recalled a scary time, when he was about three, that he got really sick. The doctors said he had brain fever and nothing could be done to save him, but Aunt Rila Farrior took a look and said not a thing was wrong with him but worms. She sent Earline to get peach tree leaves from which she made a tea and started giving it to Linwood, a little at a time. After about two hours, Lin woke up and asked for Earline. They kept giving him the peach leaf tea, and soon he was as good as new.

Family. Family held on to its tenuous ties during hard times, like that Spanish moss clutching the limbs of the big live oak trees she could see ahead of her. Spanish moss needed a tree to grow on. Family needed each other. Family that, like so many others in these days, felt the grief of early deaths. It was kinship that saw them through, across the generations.

Abraham, Mittie's father, Earline's Granddaddy Stevens, was the oldest family member she'd known. She didn't remember her grandmother, Rhoda, Granddaddy Steven's first wife who'd died giving birth to Mittie's two-years-younger sister May, but she did remember his second wife, Charity. Before her grandfather came to live with them after Charity's passing, Earline recalled their occasional visits.

On one of those visits, late at night, Charity, dressed in a long white nightgown and white nightcap, moved as quietly as she could through the little house, looking for the door out. She needed to find the outhouse. Her presence or some movement awakened Walter, and through the fog of sleep, he spied what seemed an eerie apparition dressed all in white, floating through the house. He grabbed his shotgun from where it lay by his bed and took aim. He was about to squeeze the trigger when Mittie woke up, saw what was happening, and cried, "Walter, don't point that thing at Charity!"

It took a moment for the reality to sink in, and Walter, shaking either from the fright of seeing a ghost or of almost shooting his mother-in-law, put the gun down, lay back, and breathed out a long, shuddering sigh.

Watching two squirrels chasing around the trunk of a big live oak tree, Earline thought how the humor in that story still made her smile. But one that still raised the hair on the back of her neck was the time when the sound of hooves on the hard clay road woke her late one night. The Brunson place where they lived then was a ways out of town and there were few other houses out there, and no one ever passed by that time of night.

Blinking and rubbing her eyes, Earline saw her mama across the room standing stock-still, peering through a crack in the wall, out into the darkness. Earline had to know what was out there. Rising from her bed, she padded as quietly as she could over to where her mama stood and nestled against Mittie's leg, curious about what had caught her attention so completely. Mittie put her hand out, pulled Earline to her, held her tight there. She could feel her mother's tense muscles beneath her cotton nightgown, but she could barely hear her shallow breathing. She found another crack in the warped wood wall and peered out, still staying close to her mama.

Through that crack she could see quite a bit on that warm, clear, moonlit night, and she watched as a lot of men rode down the road on horses, some singly, others grouped together, their bodies tilting forward slightly, their shoulders and heads extended as if they were animals intent on some prey. Earline was just guessing they were men, because it wasn't possible to say for sure what they were with their faces masked and bodies covered with what seemed like sheets. White sheets, draping the horses' rumps, the ends flapping with the horses' movement. Bright white in the moonlight. Must've been ice white, because seeing them chilled her to the bone as she watched them ride past the cabin and on down the clay road.

Afterwards her mama had held her tightly in her arms for a few minutes, and when they were both breathing normally, led her back to bed. Earline didn't know where those riders were going, what they were doing, or even who they were, but in later years, she learned some of them were important men. In a time and place where certain activity was accepted among those with power, those without it didn't question. As a child, there was nothing she could do, even had she known who they were or what they were doing.

Shaking those thoughts away, Earline told herself that life wasn't fair in lots of ways, but thank goodness for people like her daddy and her mama who tried to make it better.

Passing alongside a cornfield, she saw the late crops ripening in the soft sun, stirring the stew of memories from those earlier days, the gardens and their gifts. There was usually enough food, thanks to her daddy's logging and her mama's resourcefulness and hard work. Mittie kept a garden, and she'd can enough fruits and vegetables to get them through the winter. Earline helped her put up about a hundred jars of tomatoes, okra, peas, beans, pears, figs and other good things every year, even pickled peaches, although these were saved for company and picnics. And they'd had cows. One of Earline's jobs was to get the cows in and milk them, so they had fresh milk. Her favorite cow was the one that gave the most cream. She always loved creamy things, and the creamier the milk, the better.

Earline sometimes helped out by running errands into town, more than two miles round-trip. She remembered how her skinny brown arms clutched that peck of meal, those nine pounds or so of basic food the reason for the trip, making that last half mile seem mighty long. But as usual, Mr. Lanier had let her pick out a piece of

Chapter Three: Back to Memories

candy, and she sucked on it as she trudged along.

The next week she took two Rhode Island Red hens down to Mr. Liddon's Dry Goods Store. Her mama told her to trade them for a pair of shoes, and that made the trip seem even more worth her while.

She carried the hens by their feet, one in each hand, their heads just barely clearing the ground if Earline bent her elbows and held her arms up enough. Funny that the hens didn't fight you if you held them that way, upside down.

Her mama often salted down the plentiful fish her daddy and the boys caught in the river, lakes, and ponds all around. In the winter Walter would shoot ducks, which they preserved with salt. The hogs he raised would be butchered in the colder weather and then smoked in their smokehouse out back.

Walter sharecropped cotton, peanuts, corn and other vegetables on about thirty acres. After it had ripened, the corn would have to dry, then be taken in to be ground into meal. As for the peanuts, they'd shake the dirt off them and pile them around a pole so the peanuts would dry out, too. And when it was time to pick the cotton, everyone picked because they had to get it in before the rain came. She was too little then to carry the usual croker sack, so her mama made her a little flour bag to put the cotton bolls in. Mittie had planted the love of gardening in her daughter, and it would stay with her always. But Earline wouldn't miss that hard, hot work of picking cotton.

Just about every time Earline passed a garden or worked in one, she'd think of Uncle Jim Pope. Decades later when the word gained meaning, she would look back and think of him as their first "hippy," with his long beard, uncut hair, and interest in making sure everybody got the food they needed. He knew what everybody had in their gardens, and he spent his days going from one house to another, collecting whatever was most abundant in each garden and taking it to those who didn't have any of it at all. Collards, squash, tomatoes, peas—community food share embodied in Uncle Jim Pope. Earline remembered him coming up to their house, bringing her mama some greens, setting them down on the porch, then taking some squash from their patch. A good day's work—taking people food they didn't have and could certainly use. Kind of a Robin Hood of the garden.

As for supplies, a good source was the Rolling Store. Coming right to the door on certain days, that big old truck with its built-on storage area carried kerosene and lamps, thread, needles, pins, hard candy, and sometimes nice dress cloth. An especially welcome sight in the summer was the ice truck that meant they could have ice-cold lemonade. It was a special treat, getting some of the lemonade her mama made in that big pitcher, the lemonade her daddy and brothers drank as they worked all day in the fields. Walter would bring them lemons that he'd somehow managed to get, and in the fall sometimes he'd get a hank of bananas that was as tall as he was. Apples, too—a whole barrel full—so many they couldn't even eat them all; the ones that fermented he'd use to make cider.

Walking felt so good. A mockingbird flew down and perched on a fencepost as she passed, cocking its head, watching her quizzically. A little farther on she came to a pecan tree and saw someone had carved letters in the bark of one. It reminded Earline of how hoboes had come to their house, probably because those who came before had marked a trail pointing out the homes where people were friendly. When the hoboes asked for food, they'd also ask what chores they could do to help out, and Mittie usually had them cut stove wood. When they finished, she'd give them a plate of collards or turnip greens, piled high, along with some cornbread. It was no wonder the trail led to their house.

Quite a few tramped through that area, men on the move because they had no place to stay put. No homes, no jobs during the Depression and those recessions. From listening to the grown-ups talk, she knew about how hoboes sneaked rides on the train, on the top of it or in an empty boxcar. She knew when the trains stopped in Sneads, the stationmaster or the conductor usually threw them off.

Sometimes she'd seen those homeless souls walking with packs on their backs, but most often with something tied up on a stick resting over their slumped shoulders, if they had anything at all.

Sometimes Uncle Lon would bring the hoboes home. Earline suspected he wanted someone to talk to, somebody new. She remembered one man who stayed for dinner, and the whole family watched in amazement as he lined the peas up on his knife and then passed that knife through his mouth sideways, never dropping a single pea. If a man stayed through the night, Mittie gave him a quilt and a pillow so he could sleep on the porch.

But of the people passing through, Earline was most fascinated by the gypsies. Back when the family lived on the old Brunson place, about a mile up the red clay road on the north side of Sneads, the gypsies camped about a quarter of a mile away. Sometimes the women came to the house and talked with her mama. Mittie wouldn't let them in beyond the porch, but she was always friendly to them. And best of all, she'd let Earline and the other kids visit the gypsies in their camp.

She could see them now, those four or five horse-drawn wagons jingling and swaying down the road. Their arrival signaled some enthralling days for Earline. After the gypsies settled in, most often Earline and J.W. went down to visit with the women, men, and children, all dressed in such colorful clothes—women in head scarves and layers of skirts and flounces, men in their leather vests, children wearing all kinds of trousers, skirts, and shirts. She and her brother watched as if it were a performance as the gypsies built fires to cook on, talking and laughing while they worked.

Later, out would come their violins and guitars, and they'd make the music that charmed and carried Earline to another world. Music. Earline and her family weren't much used to music. No radios, concerts, bands around those parts in the late 1920s and into the 1930s. Hearing the happiness, the longing, the sweetness of those sounds enchanted them all. And there was the dancing. The gypsies twirled, clapped, stamped, kicked, leaped—the cheerfulness, the liveliness of it all making Earline's heart swell and dance with joy.

These exotic travelers were good to Earline and J.W., inviting them into their lives that way. Staying for a few days, sometimes a week, they enlivened Earline's life, sparked her curiosity and nourished her imagination about the world beyond Jackson County, Florida. She'd wondered over where they came from, where they went, why they traveled like that from place to place. In those days, all she'd ever known was life in a house. True, the family moved frequently, usually at the end of each year, but always from house to house and in the same general area. But when the gypsies moved on, there was Earline still somewhere around Sneads, living in a house.

Walking back to the house, Earline thought perhaps she knew a little more about the wandering life now that she'd been across the country. She may have even had a hint of how the pull between home and travel could tug at her own life.

CHAPTER FOUR

Heartbreak
1938–1940

WHAT WAS IT ABOUT COMING HOME THAT BROUGHT BACK memories with such force? Must have been her brothers and sisters, each so different, each special to her. Tiny, red-haired Rubye, who clung to her neck when she'd lift her up, little Jimmy with his sweet smile, young Linwood, with his bottomless brown eyes, or Uncle Lon, whom she loved and also rebelled against. There was something about being with people whose hardships through poverty and illness were yours; whose loss was your loss. It could have been the nonstop green of this semi-tropical place, so unlike the vast desert, the high plains, the majestic mountains. Was it those towering oaks that held the memories in, the breezes ruffling though the branches and leaves, reminiscences riding on the humid waves of air? Memories.

In those days, people took care of each other, and her mama had done lots of that. Earline's cousin Earl came to stay every summer, and other kids, too, whom Mittie took in for long periods when things weren't going so well in their own homes. Those were the happier times. Earline, though not one to spend a lot of time in such reflection, analyzing the deep significance of what things might mean, would come to know that those happier events and times had helped shape her, helped her see the world the way she did. But so, too, did the difficult experiences and her recollections of them.

Her daddy had developed heart problems, a sickness that began a downward spiral for the family, triggering a chain of events that would change everything. That sickness robbed Walter of his ability to work and provide for his family, even sparingly, as he'd been able to do even throughout the difficult Depression and Recession days of the 1920s and most of the '30s.

Earline would forever after think in terms of "before Daddy got sick," and "after Daddy got sick." "Before" signaled happier days, the place and time she thought of as home. "After" represented that happiness sliding away in worry, responsibility and grief, pushing her into sudden adulthood,

By the time their daddy got sick, the older boys, Red, Melvin, J.W. all had jobs, bringing in some money, helping to support the family. And soon Earline had to help out, too. She left school to work for the Southwells, the school principal and his wife. It was ironic, though that wasn't a word she used at the time, how she couldn't go to school because she was working for the principal. Earline loved school. Geography in particular was her subject. She'd always pore over her books of maps and stories, captivated by the idea of different places, different people. Even the details about which crops farmers grew in Greece and which animals the British raised interested her. People and places far away, all had taken hold in her mind.

She'd liked other things about school, too. That her friends were there to talk and laugh with, that she'd been nominated for Halloween Queen. But sadly for Earline, there'd been no money for a dress; she'd withdrawn her nomination, and the honor went to someone else. She accepted it stoically, because that was the way things were and there was nothing to be done about it. She'd just pulled herself up and gone on.

Between needing to earn money and helping out at home, there just was no time for going to school. Instead, Earline helped Mrs. Southwell with her child, with cleaning, cooking, and other

Chapter Heart: Heartbreak 1938–1940

household chores. That was another bit of irony, since Earline really didn't like housework. She would have preferred to be outside exploring, playing, or even working—as long as it was out-of-doors. But each day after finishing the day with Mrs. Southwell, she'd go home and carry on with housework there.

Adding to the family's strains over the past year, as she cared for Walter, Mittie also had been caring for Granddaddy Stevens, who was in the throes of advanced stomach cancer. She kept Granddaddy Stevens separated from the other family members in a back room, wanting to help him rest and to spare others the smells, sounds, and suffering of that illness. She looked after him until the end, 1937, when he died.

Exhausted from the demands of caring for her father, but still nursing Walter, along with keeping her large family fed and going, her mama truly needed help from her children. Earline could see it plain as day. With three little ones under the age of eight, the youngest, Rubye, only a year old, Mittie welcomed their help.

Devoted to her mama, Earline learned much about love from Mittie, through her experience of it for her and from her. To Earline, in her world of scarcity and trials, Mittie represented the word love itself. Her mama was her closest bond, her precious link to all that was kind and caring. She trusted her above all and tried hard to live up to what she taught, to her example. Therefore, working instead of going to school was bearable, because it helped her mama and the rest of her family.

At the Southwells, Earline earned a much-needed $2.50 a week. She gave two dollars to Mittie each payday and kept fifty cents for her secret savings. With that money, she intended to buy her mama a new pair of shoes, something Mittie hadn't had for a long time. When at last she had enough saved, elated, she bought the shoes. But to Earline's everlasting despair, Mittie never got to wear her new shoes.

Mittie fell ill herself, the last straw coming from washing clothes outside in the cold wind. Worn down by continual anxiety and so much hard work, she developed pneumonia. Earline stayed rooted by her bedside through the brief, ill-fated sickness. Mittie was forty-four years old when she died.

Sudden and devastating, Mittie's death destroyed sixteen-year-old Earline's trust in the world. It was a blow that sent her reeling, a wound never to be completely healed. It left a hole in her heart she would forever search to fill.

Then, just when Earline thought nothing else could hurt her, thirteen months later, her daddy died. He died from the congestive heart failure that had been plaguing him, although some said it was a broken heart that took him so soon after Mittie's passing.

Walter's older brother, her Uncle Lon, was the only one left to take care of the five younger children. A bachelor and a logging man, he was unprepared for the task, but he tried to do the best he could for the nieces and nephews he treasured. Earline, in the throes of grief, traveling those well-worn roads of anger, denial, and desolation began to feel more deeply the anxiety of adolescence. Hers had become a world marked by loss, lack of opportunity, monotony, and poverty.

So many heartbreaking memories, but so many joys back here at home. Walking these roads again after traveling across the country, looking back on all she'd lost here in this place, she wondered whether this was still home. She felt most acutely the absence of her graceful, beautiful, kind mama. She missed Granddaddy Stevens and Daddy, too. Yes, Uncle Lon and her brothers and sisters were here, and she loved them, she did, but she just wasn't sure what was home anymore. Maybe she had the wandering spirit of those gypsies; she certainly still carried the longing for adventure, which had been so well satisfied on the open road and with the carnival. Hers was the kind of imagination that forever sought possibility beyond the reality of what was.

She asked herself if it was possible to find happiness. She would spend much of her lifetime trying to answer this question, occasionally finding momentary joy in adventure or contentment in tantalizing but fleeting experiences of what could be called home.

CHAPTER FIVE

Frying Pans and Flying Machines
1940–1941

WHEN EARLINE THOUGHT BACK ON THE YEAR BEFORE SHE hitch-hiked across the country, before the dullness of life sent her out on that fateful walk, she thought of how she'd tried to make things work for her family and for herself. Taking that walk and ending up on the trip sure showed that those attempts hadn't panned out. But she had tried.

After her daddy died, she'd taken a job as a kind a of car-hop at a nearby drive-in cafe. Owned by Uncle John, not her uncle, but an old family friend, the business served what she thought of as easy food—sandwiches, hamburgers. It also sold liquor, the bottles thinly disguised in brown paper sacks.

Working at Uncle John's, she saw locals and travelers coming and going along Highway 90. When a car pulled into Uncle John's dirt drive and parked, she'd make sure she had her pad and pencil ready before going out to take the order. Most customers were polite and friendly, so at least she got to talk with different people, folks from all over. Even the doctors from the hospital over in Chattahoochee came, ordering big trays of sandwiches and expecting a bottle of Jack Daniels or Southern Comfort in its paper sack buried in the middle.

For years, Earline treasured the memory of the time Roy Acuff and the Smoky Mountain Boys, a famous country-western star and his band, stopped there. The singer and his band pulled in for a late-night snack after doing a show nearby. Acuff, known nationally as the King of Country Music, in those days was the Grand Master of the Grand Old Opry in Nashville. He was all the rage back then, so having them show up at Uncle John's was nothing short of heart-stopping.

Earline was the lucky one to take their order. She could almost feel her eyes sparkle as she turned her smile full-on and asked what they wanted.

From the driver's seat, Acuff smiled back at her. "Hey there," he said, his familiar voice sounding so warm. "Just some hamburgers. And Cokes, thanks."

Earline could hardly wait for the order to be filled so she could serve it. But once she did, she knew there was no reason to hang around. Smiling still, she gave them the check and took their money. Including a nice tip. She felt a high-wattage glow when Roy Acuff told her he thought she was "mighty nice." She thought they all were mighty nice, too, and down to earth, and she wondered what a life like theirs might be like.

While working at the drive-in, Earline met a man from North Dakota, someone who would take her life in a completely different direction—temporarily. Robert Fleek took quite a fancy to her and impressed her by promising to help take care of her younger brothers and sisters, something she cared about deeply and worried about constantly. He vowed to help in any way he could.

Flattery and attention weren't new to Earline, but Robert seemed different. He was so sincere, so persuasive. His work, which seemed in demand, but which she never quite understood, involved electrical high wires, and he traveled where the jobs took him. His father traveled with him, and for a while they were staying in Jackson County. Earline liked his father quite a lot.

Now, Earline wasn't looking for a husband, but she was seeking some sense of security for the younger ones in her family.

Chapter Five: Frying Pans & Flying Machines 1940–1941

Opportunities to provide that security for her little brothers and sisters were more than scarce. A seventeen-year-old girl, in a place where any job paid little and wasn't particularly interesting, didn't seem to have many choices. Robert offered a choice.

Several friends urged her to marry him, including older, trusted friends like Uncle John, his wife, Miss Effie, and Clyde Edwards. With their nudging in this direction, Earline began to think of marrying Robert as a way to solve several problems at once. It could be a kind of exchange where both sides got something. He would get her as his wife—the spirited beauty of Jackson County, or so he said. And she would get that longed-for security for her family.

Frustration and desperation fed her thinking. Frustration borne of no obvious alternatives. Desperation from a sense of being backed into a corner, coming out of her wish to find an immediate solution. Earline, who years later would say she wasn't the analytical type, who then as now preferred action over open-ended uncertainty, chose what seemed to her the clear solution. Despite her deeper feelings of doubt and anxiety, she determined that marrying Robert was her best course of action, perhaps the only practical choice, and that's the one she made. She would deal with consequences, she decided, when and if they came.

The couple were married in Tallahassee in a simple ceremony attended only by the minister, the groom's father, and two witnesses. Underage at seventeen, Earline had Miss Effie and Clyde to serve as witnesses and sign the marriage certificate.

The single, telling thing Earline would remember about that event was how nervous and nauseated she felt. She tried to calm herself down, but she just couldn't. Someone, Miss Effie maybe, gave her an Alka-Seltzer thinking it might soothe her nervous stomach, but, instead, it had the opposite effect, and she threw up several times. She went through with it, though; she and Robert were married. Whether from the effect of the Alka-Seltzer or the after-effects of the wedding, Earline couldn't say, but she knew she would never again take Alka-Seltzer, and she never has.

Robert's work took them to Norfolk, Virginia. There they, with his father, moved into a small apartment. It was there in Norfolk that Earline awoke to the reality of her situation. She was in a strange city, in a strange apartment, with a man she hardly knew—and was beginning to realize that she didn't even like. Rather than the relief she thought she'd feel about Robert's promise to help with the kids, she felt hemmed in, trapped. Within days, she knew she had to get out.

One morning, shortly after Robert left for work and his father was out for a walk, Earline slipped out of the apartment building and headed down a side street. She didn't know Norfolk and she didn't know which direction to go, but she knew she was going. Walking along at a fast clip, she was startled when a car stopped beside her and the driver got out. It was Robert. Although she'd tried to act as if things were normal, Robert must have sensed something was up. He'd been waiting outside the apartment building. He took her back to the apartment.

Earline, however, was not to be deterred. Several times, she made attempts to leave, each time taking a different street, going at different times of the day. After several botched efforts, Robert's father saw the hopelessness of the situation and counseled his son to take his wife back to Sneads.

His father's advice and his own interest in checking out work possibilities on down in Miami persuaded Robert to take her back home. In Sneads, they stayed on the west side of town in one of several little cabins owned by Uncle John.

As Earline suspected would happen, after only a few days, Robert wanted to move on. He told Earline it was time to leave. She balked at the idea of going farther south, and especially with Robert. He insisted. Earline took a stand. "No. I'm not going to Miami. You'll have to go without me."

Earline watched the red creep up Robert's neck, then over his face. Unbelieving, she saw his arm draw back and come toward her. The blow knocked her back against a pile of cooking utensils, sending the pans crashing to the floor. The shock of the impact, of the act itself, stunned her.

As Robert walked over to his suitcase and bent to pick up a shirt, Earline's hair-triggered temper fired. Springing to her feet, her hand closed around the handle of a cast-iron frying pan, and she went for him. With adreneline-powered strength, she raised the pan and swung it at Robert's head, making contact. Robert staggered back, crashing into the chairs and table behind him.

By this time, Uncle John had heard the ruckus and, shotgun in hand, charged into the cabin. Taking one look at Robert, he roared, "You son-of-a-bitch! You leave her alone! You get the hell out of here right now, or I'm gonna blow hell out of you!"

Robert knew Uncle John meant business, that he was protective of Earline. Pausing only long enough to grab his suitcase, Robert bolted out of the cabin. Earline later learned that once in his car and moving, he stopped only long enough to pick up her brother Red, who'd said he wanted to go south, too. The two men sped off to Miami.

Marriage, living in Norfolk, and the fight back in Sneads had all happened within three weeks. But for Earline, they were three nightmarish weeks, weeks she'd rather have spent doing almost anything else. She knew she'd made a huge mistake, despite her good intentions. Ultimately she determined to bring that misstep to an end. She would file for an annulment, but she had to find the wherewithall to do that, and that would take a little time.

Earline missed Red and was glad he didn't stay long in Miami. He'd hated the job there, climbing high up those poles, working with those crazy wires. And he couldn't stand the heat. Miami seemed hotter than Sneads, which to most people already was plenty hot. He came back and eventually, he offered Earline the fifty dollars she needed to end that mistake of a marriage. Robert, mercifully, did not return. To her great relief, Earline never saw him again.

Seventeen-year-old Earline stayed on in the cabin alone, working for Uncle John and Miss Effie. One and a half of the two dollars she earned each week went toward groceries for the family back at Uncle Lon's.

❧•❦

EVERY NOW AND THEN THINGS DO SEEM TO FALL INTO YOUR lap, good things. Whenever Earline thought of Roy Green and his flying machine, she couldn't help but smile. Roy's appearance on the scene brought a happy interlude after the mess with Robert. It would also bring a lull before a war no one yet knew the country would enter.

This happy turn she embraced, for it brought the unexpected, a hint of novelty, and a distinct contrast to the confinement she'd felt earlier. Roy, lighthearted and audacious, was nothing but fun. And he offered her a chance to make a little money.

Resourceful Roy earned a sweet living selling candy. He'd developed a pyramid set-up in which he distributed candy to interested people, mostly farmers, who then sold to others. He took a cut of the earnings to cover the cost of the candy, his expenses, and a little income for himself. Operating across a fairly wide territory over several counties in the Florida Panhandle, Roy traveled from place to place in *The Flying Machine*, his old jalopy.

He met Earline when, not long after she left Uncle John's and moved back in with the family, he stopped at her house to sell candy. Those two friendly souls easily fell into conversation and soon became chums. Roy invited Earline to go along with him on his route and help out by taking charge of money collection. Earline readily accepted.

Earline's knack for talking with people matched up nicely with Roy's creative salesmanship. The two of them made quite the team, he making the initial contacts, acquiring the candy, and keeping accounts for the business, she taking in the proceeds and further livening up those business connections. Her experience with Roy

Chapter Five: Frying Pans & Flying Machines 1940–1941

would be a primer for jobs several decades later when she would find her footing in sales. Earline loved that kind of work and was very, very good at it.

During this time in 1941, with money tight, farmers couldn't always pay the cash they owed Roy. They often had to use the little money that came their way for other, more pressing debts, debts that consistently seemed in greater supply than the hard cash to pay them. Sometimes a farmer would offer livestock as barter. Roy was always open to those exchanges, despite the occasional unexpected consequence.

Once they got a lamb in the barter. Roy and Earline drove off, with lamb in tow, laughing at the good deal they got. But soon they discovered their good deal was covered with lice and they found themselves scrambling to find delouser.

Another time a farmer gave them chickens. They figured they'd have one for dinner and went to a nearby creek to prepare their feast. Deciding on a good plump one, they gathered kindling and wood to build a fire for roasting it, thinking to let the fire burn down a bit while they butchered and dressed the hen. It was when they were both squatting down, laying the wood for the fire, when they heard *bock, bock, bock* coming from what seemed all around them. They turned toward the cage to see the chickens had somehow gotten loose and were high-tailing it off as fast as their legs would take them. Some fled to the north into dense bushes, some to the south through briar patches, yet others went to the east and west. Roy and Earline, running in opposite directions, chased that flock of good deals through trees, bushes, and briars, finally catching almost all of them.

Restless, feisty Earline thought Roy's friendship was the perfect remedy for temporarily forgetting the ups and downs of the last few years. She appreciated the lightness of spirit and positive outlook Roy brought into her life. And she sure had fun with their little adventures, especially the one with the piglet and sow.

It happened when they were on their longer rounds, collecting money and re-supplying their customers. Driving the sixty miles or so to Panama City on long, lonesome Highway 20, they made up riddles and told jokes to pass the time. As they drove down the deserted two-lane highway, a road framed by the panhandle's abundant pine forests, they spotted a baby pig at the edge of the brush. Unable to resist the idea of getting that little pig, Roy pulled over and parked the car.

Jumping out of the Flying Machine and dashing across the road, with admirable skill Roy managed to grab the unsuspecting piglet before it could run away. The piglet squealed like crazy; twisting and wiggling, it struggled to get free. But Roy held on tight. He was determined to get it to the car where Earline stood, laughing and enjoying the show.

At that moment a huge shape came crashing through the bush, heading straight for Roy. Mama sow. She wanted her baby back, and she wanted it now.

Quick to react, Earline hopped into the car and locked the door. Roy ran back across the road toward the car as fast as he could, but the sow was gaining on him. Refusing to let the piglet go, he held it tight as he tried to pull open the car door. He soon realized he couldn't get in the locked door, which Earline refused to unlock. Still holding the piglet, he managed to crawl on top of the car where he sat for a moment trying to catch his breath. He was still determined to have that piglet. But his determination was matched by mama sow's. She was squealing and jumping up against the car, making it rock, creating something of a porcine-human stand-off.

Within minutes, as if in response to the commotion, several other piglets streamed out of the bush, too, all squealing at the top of their lungs. With all that ruckus assaulting his ears and the sow's fierce resolve becoming increasingly clear, Roy finally admitted defeat and put the piglet down. He hated that. He'd wanted that piglet so bad. But then, so had its mama.

Chapter Five: Frying Pans & Flying Machines 1940–1941

The delightful interval with Roy would remain among Earline's fond memories of that time. But situations change, good times come to an end, often all too soon. In 1941, the U.S. had entered the war, and Roy, like so many others, had gone off to fight in it. And then Earline, again prey to the boredom of the everyday life there in Sneads, had taken off on that unplanned trip across the country.

But now, here she was again, right back in Jackson County, wondering what was next.

Chapter Six

Adventures of a Different Kind

In some ways Earline felt as if she'd never left, never traveled those thousands of miles, never been part of a carnival, had only dreamed extraordinary dreams about having amazing adventures. In Jackson County, everything felt unchanged. Against the backdrop of war— that major war that had drawn almost all of the young men away, including Melvin and J.W.— she felt suspended in time. She was anxious about the boys who were away. She was anxious about life in general. Her days passed in a dreary procession, and she could hardly stop her fretting.

Movies were her single distraction. Earline was always happy to settle into one of the padded seats with her popcorn and Coca-Cola and wait to be carried away from the tiresomeness of everyday life. She looked forward to the moment when the thick curtains would slowly part, revealing the screen, as the projector whirred from back of the small balcony behind the audience sending out light and sound in a dust-mote filled stream.

First came trumpeting music and a deep, resonant voice announcing the MovieTone newsreel. There were images of that distant war, and of their boys who were fighting it. Wavering between pride and fear, Earline watched soldiers march, airplanes fly, and ships sail, often in places she'd never even heard of before.

Following the news came the previews of coming attractions,

whetting her movie appetite for more, always more. Then the cartoons and Mickey, Goofy, or Elmer Fudd to make Earline laugh. Finally, the main attraction. Eyes glued to the screen and ears on the alert, Earline took in every frame of Clark Gable, Gene Autry, or Vivien Leigh, every word they spoke. Lost in their stories, she became the hero or heroine who did and said just the right thing, taking the unheard of risk just in the nick of time.

The movies restored Earline for a time, but she wished she could go more often, though she appreciated Red's taking her almost once a week. They'd usually go to the late show because of Red's having to work. Sometimes friends would go with them, like Rog, who liked Earline a lot. Protective Red was certain to be there whenever Rog went along.

It was after the late show in Chattahoochee one August night, about midnight, when she, Red and Rog started out for home, Rog driving. A deep southern darkness clothed the night. They rode along laughing and talking about the movie when, out of the dark, a pair of oncoming lights swerved across the line toward them, sideswiping their car and forcing them off the road. They bumped to a stop on the grassy roadside. While Red and Rog jumped out, Earline stayed behind in the car, trying to catch her breath. The swerve and then the impact had thrown her against the steering wheel, knocking the breath out of her.

The offending car stopped on the other side of the road. Behind them, cars pulled over. Other movie-goers, who'd seen the accident, wanted a look at what was going on. Earline heard shouting and turned to see a face in the window beside her. Mag Hawk, a person she knew only by sight, stood screaming at her, spitting out the sounds. "You dumb bitch! You were driving and you ran into us!"

Mag's words were slurred, soaked in the stench of alcohol.

Earline popped out of the car. *Nobody* could talk to her like that. Mag grabbed, and with a vicious jerk, pulled Earline toward her. Earline didn't know how it happened, but the next thing she did

Chapter Six: Adventures of a Different Kind

know, she was in the middle of Highway 90, sitting on top of Mag, banging the drunk's head against the pavement. Then, in a single, surprising move, Mag grabbed Earline's hair, yanked her head down, and sank her teeth into Earline's neck.

That hurt, maybe even more than her scalp from the pulled hair that gave real meaning to that old southern expression "snatch you baldheaded." There Earline was, hair clamped in Mag's left hand, her neck under Mag's right. Held tight and in close, up against her torso, only one move seemed possible, and she made it. Earline open her mouth wide, clamped down and ground her teeth with all her might—right into Mag's looming breast.

Mag screamed, furious, and bellowed, "You sonofabitch! You bit my titty off!"

The crowd around them roared, titillated by the crazy show. When a Sneads policeman arrived and in an instant summed up the situation, he yelled at Red, "You'd better get Earline off Mag, or I'll have to take both of 'em to jail."

Big, six-foot-two-inch Red, who'd been watching the action along with everyone else, obliged and, with some reluctance, pulled Earline off Mag as easily as a kid picking up a toy. With one arm he held the kicking, twisting Earline off the ground, thinking maybe she needed to work off some of that steam. Earline's arms and legs flailed furiously. Her cowboy boots, a souvenir of her trip west, were a whirring blur. On one of those wild kicks, the toe of Earline's boot made contact with Mag's jaw, making a sickening crunch.

Again Mag screamed, this time yelling, "You sonofabitch. You broke my jaw!"

The crowd of spectators, pretty sizable by then, jumped up and down, cheering, yelling encouragement to Earline.

Word got out about the ruckus, about how Earline when goaded, had given Mag a serious beating. Everyone knew Mag, the aggressive bully who picked on anybody, and especially on those who couldn't fend for themselves. People laughed when they thought about how

Mag had finally picked the wrong target. For weeks after, Earline couldn't walk down the street in Sneads without someone wanting to buy her a Coca-Cola. In a town of about a thousand, Earline felt like almost every person in it must've bought her a Coke.

The occasional eruption of excitement did little, though, to answer Earline's deep need for a purpose, for a way to take her beyond what she already knew and had already experienced. Her days crawled by as she cast about for ways to fill them.

Waking on a morning that promised to be just like all the others, Earline couldn't know that, in fact, that one day would change the course of her life.

Red had awakened with a splitting headache. When he discovered his usual remedy, a dope or doping—aspirin washed down with a Coke—wasn't on hand, he asked Earline to walk to the little store and get them.

She strode to the little juke-joint down on Highway 90 and got the aspirin and Coke, then turned right around and started back home. But she'd barely left the store when she spotted an odd scene that made her pause. Smack in the middle of the eastbound side of the road, there were a car, a man, and one massive dead hog.

Having taken it all in, Earline marched up to the man standing in the road beside the car. "You hit that hog!" she said to him.

From under his Panama hat, deep brown eyes took her in. One hand on her hip, the other holding a Coke and a box of aspirin, she looked from him to the dead hog lying in front of his car.

He said in an even voice, "That hog walked out in front of me. I didn't have time to stop." His jaw tightened slightly. "You can see there's a ditch on this side of the road and too much traffic on the other to have gone around him."

Earline felt bad about the hog. And not liking to give up her point of view so easily, she felt a little bad that the man's explanation sounded reasonable.

There was a lot of traffic on the westbound side of the road and

Chapter Six: Adventures of a Different Kind

no shoulder. No fence laws existed in those days and, not wanting or being able to take on extra expense, a lot of people didn't bother to put them up. That put the hog in the road, dead, and blocking traffic.

Now that she'd taken the time to take in his side of the story, she could see that the hog-killer probably had little choice in the matter. He was a pleasant-faced fellow who spoke with an accent not of those parts. She felt herself relenting a little.

While they'd been talking, several cars and trucks had stopped behind the man's. Three local men, all clad in well-worn overalls, came over to find out what was going on. After sizing up Earline and the driver, they offered to drag the hog from the road. One of them knew the owner, who lived nearby, and volunteered to relay the news of his hog's fate.

As the men went about their work, Earline and the man in the Panama hat stood talking in the bright morning son. At home, Red's headache throbbed on as Earline learned the man's name was Bob Wilson.

Within minutes the hog had been pulled over into the ditch and Bob could move his car. Traffic was flowing again, but Bob didn't go far. He pulled his car over a few yards on, parked, got out and walked back to where Earline was still standing. Clearly, they hadn't finished their conversation.

"Where're you going?" she asked.

"Back to Wakulla. I bartend at Wakulla Gardens."

Earline knew the area well. Wakulla County lay south of Tallahassee, about sixty miles from Sneads. A couple years ago, just before her daddy died, she'd stayed in Monticello, a few miles away, with her friend Pauline's family. And she even knew Wakulla Gardens, a popular restaurant and bar.

"That's not where you're from. You have a funny accent."

Smiling, he explained, "No. I'm from New York. Spent some of my younger days in Scranton, Pennsylvania."

"That where you're coming from now?"

"New York, yes, and for the last time. I won't go there again." Then abruptly, "You want a ride home?"

She remembered Red's headache, and although she lived close by, she said yes.

The short drive gave her time to learn more about Bob's recent trip. He'd driven to New York for his father's funeral, but before he'd arrived, his brothers had gone ahead with the funeral. His father's brother Joe, a rug importer in New York, had been part of that decision, too. It was the final straw for him, Bob explained. An explosive argument over that decision led to a split in the family, and Bob had vowed never to communicate with his family again.

But where the argument with his brothers and uncle deepened old wounds, severing familial ties, meeting Earline hinted at something new. Before Bob left Earline's house, they agreed to see each other again, and soon. It was to be not only soon, but often.

Over the next few weeks, they learned more about each other's lives. She came to appreciate the difficulties he'd been through—how his mother died of breast cancer, soon after his youngest brother, Mickey, was born; how all three boys went to live with different relatives, Bob with a family in Scranton, Pennsylvania; how Bob had kept the deep ties to his father, who lived in New York.

When he joined the Army at sixteen, Bob had still kept in close touch with his father, even as he did later when he worked at various jobs in Chicago and Florida. Then his father died, and they had the funeral without him.

Earline could understand, gathering that his father had been Bob's strongest emotional link to family and how devastating his death must have been. Images of her mama rose in her mind. She knew that kind of loss.

In years to come, Earline would wonder about Bob's brothers, saddened that she'd never met them, didn't really know who they were or exactly where they lived—other than in the massive,

Chapter Six: Adventures of a Different Kind

anonymous city of New York. To her knowledge, there never was any communication with them, although somehow Bob did get word early the next year, 1943, when Mickey was killed on Guadalcanal.

Visiting Pauline down that way, Earline engineered a stop at Wakulla Gardens. There she saw for herself what a skillful bartender Bob was. He could mix any kind of drink, and he obviously liked people. She saw him joking with his customers, teasing them, the way he did with her. And of course, they loved it when he balanced a chair on his nose or juggled a few empty beer bottles. Earline laughed along with them. The best, though, was the chicken walk. With crooked elbows akimbo, he pranced around with knees bent and squawked in time with the lively music.

Life had become fun again.

Earline knew she intrigued Bob with her willingness to walk into any new situation, to talk to anybody. Though she was seventeen years younger than he, they'd had lots of similar adventures, and they brought that sense of adventure and daring to their quickly flowering relationship. She'd traveled with a carnival, he'd been with Ringling Brothers. She played Electra to his circus clown. She'd woven herself around swords, he'd juggled hats and batons. In her carnival days, she'd played her different parts, but Bob was still the all-around entertainer. He'd traveled much of the country, too. Landing in Florida seemed to suit him just fine; he'd stayed.

He also had a knack for attracting opportunities in this undeveloped area, one he thought of as being ripe with possibility. Though it wasn't one to be counted on, this knack would play out in positive ways over a decade or more.

Earline and Bob were two people who seemed to click. Before long they wove together the common threads in their lives—unconventional backgrounds, an interest in creating something for themselves out of life, along with a willingness to cast their lot with fate. Only a few months elapsed from the dead hog in the road, the day

Red's headache changed everything, to their marriage, and within the year they were planning a business for themselves, as well as starting a family.

Chapter Seven

Family Matters

Just as in the movies when the calendar pages fly off the wall into the blue, so did Earline feel time flying by. So much happened so quickly. Big, important things. So different from when the days dragged following her trip and before she met Bob.

The only resemblance to her pre-Bob, pre-married life in Sneads was in the moving. They moved around quite a bit, from one tiny, old place to another—broken-down houses, cabins. That part was hard. Money was scarce, with Bob now in partnership with Uncle John at the drive-in and store, and them saving as much as they could. But they were happy and knew their dreams would take some time to develop, to show any promise. For the time, they managed the best they could, keeping their sights on the future. And before too long, that future included another family member.

Born in 1943, Bruce brought a new and heart-warming dimension to their lives. That package of healthy lungs and brown eyes delighted Earline and Bob, bringing both joy and fresh challenges to their already full lives. Bruce was a lively, fussy handful. Before long he would mirror Earline's mischievous personality and more than a trace of Bob's outgoing good humor.

As for challenges, Earline's health was declining. The many big changes over the past five years had piled up—the devastating loss of her parents, the war and her brothers enlisting, travel, marriage and family; they were all catching up with her. She was having difficulty coping with the ups and downs, the juggling of uncertainties, the complexities of life. By the time Bruce passed his first birthday, Earline's high-strung nerves had frayed to the breaking point. Her doctor was concerned.

"Take Earline away for a while," he told Bob. "She needs a break."

Both Bob and Earline knew that she and travel were a good mix, and they knew that the sooner they got away, the better. Feeling the urgency to act, Bob bought an Airstream trailer. They quickly packed up and headed west on Highway 90, bound for the beaches of Corpus Christi.

Bob drove, the big, silver, bullet-shaped trailer gliding along behind the car, while Earline held Bruce on her lap. Earline and Bruce watched the passing trees, the cows, and billboards, with warm air blowing pleasantly through the open window, mussing his little bit of hair. Occasionally Bruce pointed at a passing sight, babbling and laughing. Earline and Bob laughed with him. When he pointed to a familiar billboard and said clearly, "Coca-Cola," the astonished parents could only stare in wonder. Their boy had spoken his first real word.

To be moving, going somewhere felt good to Earline. Getting away from their temporary, cramped quarters was a relief. She enjoyed every mile that passed, every landmark encountered. "Welcome to Alabama," "Welcome to Mississippi," "Welcome."

That Airstream trailer was just fine, up-to-date with a kitchen, eating area and sleeping spaces. The one flat tire caused trouble enough. Not long into Louisiana, outside the town of Slidell on the north shore of Lake Pontchartrain, they felt an ominous bump and wobble, and their investigation confirmed the bad news. One of the trailer's tires was shot, and this presented a major problem. With the War still raging, the major supplies of rubber were going to the war effort. Extra tires were scarce, and new tires were out of the question. But calling upon his wheeling, dealing resourcefulness, Bob somehow

Chapter Seven: Family Matters

managed to find a used tire, and the family continued their journey.

But Earline and Bob struggled continually with the beds. They worked with diligence to put them together securely, but those beds just wouldn't stay configured the way they were supposed to. They'd fall apart right under a sleeping person. And even if they did somehow stay together through a night, they were small with thin, lumpy mattresses. Earline tossed and turned all night, every night.

Stopping first in Metairie, on New Orleans' outskirts, they visited Aunt Bunch and Uncle Jack. Earline felt joy in seeing her daddy's older and beloved cousin and her dapper, soft-spoken husband. She sank into the love and warmth Aunt Bunch and Uncle Jack offered, breathed in their care and concern for her. She took great pleasure in being pampered and fussed over by the two of them. And she had nothing but appreciation for sleeping in a comfortable bed.

One morning shortly after they'd arrived, Aunt Bunch announced, "Earline, you and I are going out to lunch while the boys take care of Bruce. We'll need to leave at eleven to catch the downtown trolley."

At eleven sharp, Aunt Bunch, in tailored suit, smart open-toed high heels, and perky hat cocked to the right, complete with a bit of netting over the front, stood in the entryway, touching up her fashionable bright red lipstick. Pulling on her white gloves, she gave Earline an appreciative glance. Earline, wearing a flattering jersey knit dress that complimented her figure, pulled on white gloves of her own. Going out with Aunt Bunch ranked high on the list of special treats. Aunt Bunch looked for just the right parasols for them, because no lady ever left the house without her parasol.

Earline took in everything about Aunt Bunch, watching her with admiration as they boarded the trolley. What a treasure this wonderful woman was. She and Uncle Lon were the only two still living from the family's older generation, from her daddy's family. And she was the only one who'd had real polish. She admired the older woman's self-confidence, her genteelly forthright manner. And she was so fun-loving. Fishing for a compliment or an actual fish, Aunt Bunch loved a good time and was generous with her smiles and laughter.

The two smartly dressed women headed for Morrison's, Aunt Bunch's favorite, in downtown New Orleans. Riding the trolley to and from the restaurant, they chatted and gossiped like the confidants they were, oblivious to other passengers or the trolley's clang at each stop. Earline sighed, contented. This really was a vacation.

They stayed with Aunt Bunch and Uncle Jack for a week, then set off for Lake Charles to visit Earl, one of Aunt Bunch's two sons, and his wife, Flo. Earl was about seven years older than Earline, closer to Red's age. When he was young, he'd come stay with Earline's family every summer. Mittie had been particularly close to the boy, loving how he fit in with the family, teasing everyone, getting into mischief with Red, always asking Mittie to make gravy for him. In fact, Mittie had fashioned Earline's name from her favorite nephew's. To the adult Earline, visiting Earl seemed like getting gravy for herself. Cream for her soul, further soothing her ragged nerves. She'd always looked up to him, and now just being around him, being reminded of good times in her youth and of her mama's special affection for this young man, further revived her spirits.

After visiting Earl and Flo, the little family, trailer still in tow, drove to Corpus Christi, Texas. Water. The beach. Travel and large bodies of water were the elixir Earline sought, then and in the future. For several weeks, the Gulf of Mexico's calming sounds lulled and nurtured Earline, Bob, and their toddler son. It soaked them in its warm, clear waters, its saltiness keeping them afloat on its gentle and more robust waves. Earline, a master floater, loved indulging in this peaceful activity. Listening to the sea gull sounds spill through the surf's roar, digging her feet into sun-drenched sand, and teaching Bruce to build sand castles, she felt herself relax, allowed the tension to seep out of her tired body, felt the nourishing rays bake and heal her nerve endings. They kept their trailer parked in the spaces on the

Chapter Seven: Family Matters

beach and enjoyed every sparkling day.

Funny how getting away can make going home easier and provide the impetus for long-sought changes. Back in Sneads, Earline and Bob didn't just settle into their old lives. They took some big steps, steps that would take them closer to their dreams of family and financial stability. The first was buying a home of their own.

The big old Pope house was of a type that grew out of the rural South's agricultural heritage. Common during the early decades of the 1900s, it was what Earline and others called "tobacco barn style." Simple and functional, it was made of unpainted wood, which, thanks to time and weather, had developed a soft gray patina. Sitting about three or four feet off the ground, its steps led up to the front door, which opened into spacious, high-ceilinged rooms. The interior walls echoed those outside, different only in that their protection from sun, wind and rain had kept them looking younger than their outside cousins. Welcoming and big enough, at the time it was just right for Earline, Bob and their growing family. Earline loved it.

Sitting three or four hundred feet north of the red clay road on nine acres of land, the Pope house was in plain view of the old Brunson place and that little house where Earline had spent some happy childhood years. On the property's other end, in the southeastern corner, Bob would soon build a business of his own. First a building that would serve as a restaurant, with a juke box and a room big enough for dancing; also small cabins, which would house workers. Many of those workers would come to the area for the big dam project that would begin in a few years, and only a mile away. The Rivers and Harbors Act of 1946, authorized by Congress, would bring the Jim Woodruff Lock and Dam project, jobs and prospects to the area, and Bob would cash in big-time on the opportunity.

From 1950 to 1957, he would have all of the lucrative concession rights for the project—sandwiches, beverages, snacks, cigarettes. And during the early 1950s, he and Earline would buy land and build a subdivision, for which Earline would design floor plans for the first houses. Three streets would carry their children's names, and the subdivision itself would be called BruCaSue. All of this lay in the future, and it would call for a great deal of imagination, many long hours, and a lot of effort.

But now at the end of 1944, Earline and Bob found their family growing again. This time they had a daughter. Round, brown, practically hairless, Carol soon showed signs of Earline's determination and Bob's knack with language. Later Earline would describe this little child as solemn. But she was also an experimenter, even as a baby. As a favorite midnight activity, she'd stand in her crib, hold the railing with one hand and her bottle of milk or juice in the other. Throwing the bottle over the rail and watching as it shattered across the floor, she'd announce with noisy glee, "Damn bottle bwok."

Bottle after bottle submitted to her experiments, always with the same result. Earline, at her wits end, asked the doctor what to do. "Let her drink from a cup," he told her.

To Earline's amazement, it worked. No more broken bottles, and no more joyful swearing from her little girl.

Shortly after Carol was born, Earline's attention turned to something that had long been on her mind—her youngest sister, Rubye, now seven years old. Rubye had been only fifteen months old when their mother died, and Earline had long wished for the means through which she could offer Rubye a home. Now that they had one with enough space, the time seemed ripe to ask Rubye to live with them. Of her two younger siblings, Jimmy was in Jacksonville with Betty, and Rubye had been living with Red and Margaret, just outside Sneads.

Six and a half decades later, at Earline's eighty-sixth birthday party, Rubye would tell of how that came to pass and what it meant to her. Earline wouldn't have fully realized the tremendous impact it made on Rubye, nor would she have understood that in Rubye's mind, the move came out of the blue, a complete surprise. And Rubye couldn't have known that such a change had been niggling at

Chapter Seven: Family Matters

Earline for some time.

Earline worried about Rubye, about her living with Red and Margaret, who, both working at full-time jobs, weren't prepared to take care of a child. Earline's worry extended to Red and Margaret, too. She could see there was little money, almost no time or energy, and no experience at all, for raising that sad, lonely little girl.

So Earline, now at age twenty-two, acted. Moved by whatever mechanism it is that always catapulted her into action, Earline called Red and Margaret. She told her oldest brother and sister-in-law that she and Bob wanted Rubye to come live with them. Red and Margaret readily agreed it would be for the best. Earline then appeared at the school to talk with the principal. Again, she found agreement on both the difficulties of the situation and her proposed solution.

Earline knew that it was close to the end of the school day, but her impatience to have Rubye with her had grown in proportion to the steps she'd taken and she wanted the matter finished. She wanted immediate evidence that it was settled. Trying to remain calm, she held the principal's eye said, "I'd like to take Rubye home now."

The principal nodded. "Yes. I think that's a good idea."

Earline hurried down the hall to Rubye's second-grade classroom. Not minding that she was interrupting the class, she tapped on the door, opened it and stuck her head in. Her eyes immediately went to Rubye. She saw the surprised look on Rubye's face as she walked to her little desk. Kneeling down to meet Rubye's eyes, Earline said, "I'd like for you to come live with us."

She watched Rubye's eyes widen and her mouth open. Earline thought she could've knocked her little sister over with the proverbial feather.

They walked hand in hand out through the school doors and to the car. Rubye later told Earline she assumed they'd head straight for Earline and Bob's big, old house. But Earline had something else in mind. Instead of driving toward home, they turned west on Highway

90, toward Marianna, twenty miles away.

Earline could see Rubye's little forehead wrinkle, freckles peeking from the furrows, her head cocked in puzzlement as they parked in front of the one department store in the town. She took Rubye by the hand and led her into the store. It wasn't huge as department stores went, but it was bigger than any store that Rubye had ever seen. As they entered, Earline again watched Rubye's eyes grow wide as they took in row after row, shelf atop shelf filled with merchandise.

"Where did all of this come from?" the little girl asked. "I didn't know there were this many things in the world."

Coats, dresses, shoes, boots, trousers, jackets, perfume, cosmetics and heavens knows what else. Earline sensed Rubye's astonishment, but she didn't grasp the life-long impact that what happened next would have on Rubye.

Earline sifted through a rack of dresses and Rubye stood watching. Earline pulled out a soft blue dress. "Would you like to try this on?"

Rubye nodded, and Earline hung the dress on a nearby rack. As Earline held up each possibility, Rubye nodded, more vigorously each time. A green plaid dress, a pink one, one that had pearly buttons on the front.

In the little fitting room Rubye tried on each lovely dress. They picked out several they both liked, then dropped them at the counter and moved on to coats and shoes. Earline's heart swelled to see how thrilled and disbelieving Rubye seemed to be. She ached for her little sister, her sister who'd never had new things, only hand-me-downs—clothes that were serviceable, but never pretty. As a child, Earline hadn't had many herself, but at least she'd had her mama for a while, and her mama had seen to it that Earline got something special, like shoes, when she could manage it.

Earline couldn't resist putting the icing on that magical cake. She also thought children should have toys if possible, and Rubye had none. After paying for the clothes and storing them in the car,

Earline took Rubye to Woolworth's. There they bought a doll, a coloring book, and crayons. Especially for Rubye, all for Rubye. Earline had touched her little sister's heart deeply, and in a way she'd never forget. Indeed, Rubye felt she now had a home. And Earline was satisfied that finally Rubye had come to live with her, that she would be a part of the family.

≫•≪

THE THIRD CHILD AND SECOND DAUGHTER, SUSAN, ARRIVED five years later in 1949. Mischievous Bruce and experimental Carol had not prepared Earline for the burst of frenetic human energy that was Susan. This child redefined determination and matched her mother's willfulness inch for headstrong inch. If she set her sights on doing something, she did it, or screamed bloody murder when thwarted.

Susan resisted confinement, even in clothes. Given the opportunity, she would shed clothing faster than a chameleon changes color. In desperation, beleaguered helper Alice began sewing Susan's corduroy overall straps to her shirt to keep the clothing on her. Later Rosa Lee, a source of help and friendship over many years, would use safety pins for the same purpose.

Susan adored her big brother, and once she could walk, she tried to follow him everywhere. Even to school, a mile away. Once, three-year-old Susan made it all the way down that red clay road to the schoolhouse before a frantic Earline and equally anxious Rosa Lee could find the resolute tot. She wanted to be with her Bubba. Some five and a half decades later, Rosa Lee would still chuckle over Susan's determined antics.

In 1950, the home Earline and Bob had been planning and building on their property was ready for them. Designed by Earline, it would serve the needs of a family of six and offer a good gathering place for the extended family—her brothers, sisters, their spouses and children.

Sitting about a hundred yards from the old Pope house, the

new home was Sneads's first brick house. White wrought-iron work graced the front porch, azalea bushes and honeysuckle vines embraced the house's entry and sides. Inside were gleaming hardwood floors, a living room with French doors, dining room, three bedrooms, two baths, a big screened-in porch, called a Florida room, and a wood-paneled hallway. On the property were magnolia, pecan, pear, and fig trees and ample space for a vegetable garden and a chicken coop.

Earline was now settled in her new home, which she and Bob had furnished beautifully. She devoted her time to raising her children, making beautiful clothes and special-occasion costumes for them and sometimes for their cousins, Betty's daughters. She was active at the school as homeroom mother, helping with school carnivals and other activities, always ready to provide home-baked, elaborately decorated cookies and cupcakes. She loved making a home for her family, and she was determined to provide a steady diet of the kinds of broadening experiences and opportunities that she had gained only serendipitously. Creating a strong foundation for her children, she also was vicariously filling in some life experiences for herself.

She enrolled them in dancing lessons, something Carol loved, Susan tolerated, but Bruce hated. Eventually, Earline allowed Bruce to opt out, but Susan and Carol had no doubts about continuing. Earline made sure her girls had pretty dresses and costumes for their many recitals—tulle, sequins, taffeta, and ribbons all fell under the spell of Earline's sewing artistry. A piano and accompanying lessons awaited her children, and Earline put her talent to work again on perfect recital dresses for her girls. Again, Bruce gave it a try, but playing the piano just couldn't compete with gigging frogs.

A hub for the extended family, it was a rare Sunday that Earline's home wasn't full of her brothers, sisters-in-law and their kids. Even Bob would sometimes take a little time from his all-consuming work to be with the family.

A few years earlier Earline's older brothers J.W. and Melvin had

Chapter Seven: Family Matters

returned from World War II. Melvin, in search of a young woman he'd fallen in love with, had re-enlisted and gone back to Germany to find her, serving that time as a chauffeur. Unable to find his love, after his tour of duty ended he returned home, broken hearted. But after some time, Melvin sometimes joined the family, and eventually he found a mate there at home who also became part of those gatherings. Earline welcomed Edna along with her other sisters-in-law, as she did when widower Red married Willie Mae in 1953, and eight years later, when Linwood and Joanne married.

Betty and Jack, because they lived farther away, Betty east in Jacksonville and Jack west in DeFuniak Springs, were less frequently a part of the family gatherings. But they came occasionally, and those visits were special. Betty brought her nieces and nephew little gifts. Jack and his wife Mary Alice brought stacks of comic books for the kids—luxuries Mary Alice got as extras from the drug store where she worked.

J.W. and his wife, Lou, had been raising three of the cousins, three of Betty's four daughters, Beverly, Jo, and Brenda, for a number of years. Jeannie, the youngest, lived in Jacksonville with Betty and family friend, Flagg, and also later when Betty met and married Al. Susan and Carol spent much of their spare time with those cousins, Beverly being Carol's age, and Brenda, Susan's. Jo fell in between and alternately joined in the younger- or older-girl activities. Bruce often sought out the uncles to hunt and fish, endeavors that were beyond Bob's realm, but were at the heart of Earline's brothers J.W., Melvin and Linwood's worlds.

Earline was happy having family around. She welcomed little Beverly, Jo, and Brenda for overnights with Susan and Carol, just as Lou embraced the girls' overnights with her and J.W. Earline's nieces called her Aunt Jean, because at one time during her late teen-age years she had fancied the name Jean and had called herself that.

In various combinations, Earline and Lou watched the girls play hopscotch, drawing squares in the red dirt road in front of the yard or in the sandy road that ran by Lou and J.W.'s house, out a few miles from Sneads. What they didn't see was that under the huge oaks, dripping with chigger-infested moss, the girls would sometimes pause to bury the small, deceased creatures they found—tiny lizards, birds, bumblebees even, taking turns leading solemn ceremonies for the dear departed creatures.

One day when Lou and the girls were at Earline's for the day, Susan and Jo walked down the clay road pulling Susan's little red wagon. About fifty yards down, they spied a flattened polecat in the middle of the road. Wanting to do the right thing for it, they lifted the stiff, compressed carcass and put it in the wagon, intending to take it home for a proper funeral.

The little procession made its somber way up the road. As the girls with their burden turned in at the drive, Earline and Lou saw them moving deliberately and slowly toward the house. Their progress was so slow, the odor reached the women before the procession did.

"Girls! What's in that wagon?"

"It's a polecat, Aunt Jean. A poor, dead polecat." Jo said. Then she added, "I know it's a polecat because it smells just like one."

Horrified, Earline and Lou sprang into action. The molding creature, in fact a cat, never did have its funeral, but the girls did get a scrubbing with soap and hot water. It took several rounds to rid them of the polecat smell, but they persisted, also scrubbing away their girls' interest in animal funerals.

Immersed in family, Earline saw the days continue to fly by. It had taken determination and effort to create this home, this way of life. But determination and effort couldn't keep things the same. For the present, she was happy being settled, raising her family. But some of that would soon change.

CHAPTER EIGHT

A Turning Point

Sometimes it takes a bad experience to make us realize that our familiar environment is becoming less familiar, that the place we've always called home feels less comfortable. The friendliness may still be there, tricking us into complacency, but something else pushes up under and around it. And that something else began to catch Earline's attention. She could tell from the increasing reports of fights, knifings, gambling, and drunkenness that Sneads was getting rougher. It wasn't surprising given that after the war ended, the young veterans, many still haunted by their war experience, came home with little money in their pockets to face Jackson County's scant job opportunities. Joblessness and idleness make a bleak combination. Despair can cause a place to change, and over the years, it did. It wasn't surprising, nor was it reassuring.

One incident in particular horrified Earline, and it happened to someone she knew. Late in the night, a man, a combat veteran, accused of not paying a gambling debt, was beaten almost to death, then tied to the railroad track. She and Bob had heard the four a.m. train whistle, blowing time after time and for longer than they'd ever heard. They hadn't known what it meant at the time, but they soon learned.

Another night, burglars broke into Bob's restaurant and took the safe, a safe that had taken five men to carry in. Earline could only think it must have taken five to get it out. They hauled it about a mile up the road to a clearing and blew the top off, most likely with dynamite. All of the cash and four of the five pistols stored in it went missing, pistols Bob had recently shown to some of his customers. The fifth pistol was the only one Bob had registered. The burglars were never caught.

Like most mothers, Earline was fiercely protective of her children. She was a lioness when her family was concerned, and her instinctual senses were now on higher alert. The corruption and meanness were getting too close to home for her, and an episode one night in 1952 confirmed this. The incident also caused her ferociousness and courage to become legendary in the county.

Earline had put six kids to bed—Bruce, Susan, Carol, and cousins Beverly, Brenda, and Jo. Rubye was staying overnight with a friend, and Bob had been working late. Having slipped into a pattern of almost constant work, he often slept in one of his little cabins out back of the restaurant after closing up shop in the late hours. He was sleeping there that night.

Around midnight a sound awakened Earline. Looking back, she couldn't be sure whether it was the doorbell or a knock on the door, but despite her grogginess, she felt the need to investigate. She heaved herself out of bed and pulled on her robe.

Clustered together, the three bedrooms sat back and to the side of the long parquet hallway that led to the front door. Looking around the corner and down the hall, Earline could see a figure through one of the small windows at the top of the polished wood door. There was a man motioning with his hand, signaling her to come out.

Her thoughts went immediately to a family that had moved in across the road, into that little old house across the road where she'd lived in as a child. It was one of the few houses nearby. Earline wondered if maybe one of the kids there was sick and motioned for him to go around to the back of the house. She figured she could talk to him through the screen of the Florida room without letting him in.

Chapter Eight: A Turning Point

Standing by the back door that led onto the screened porch, she listened carefully and grew uneasy as he spoke. His words seemed muffled, random, and she couldn't understand. The longer he went on, the more his tone, his jumbled and rambling words, frightened her. To put some distance between the man and herself, she moved as fast as she could toward the center of the house. With her heart pounding and her hands shaking, she tried to take breaths to calm herself.

At her sudden movement, she'd seen the man run off into the darkness. Earline reached the telephone, dialed and waited for Mr. Stone to answer. Mr. Stone, the local policeman, was the only nearby help, since the sheriff was twenty miles away in Marianna. It seemed forever before she heard his voice. When she did, her words came spilling out, urgent and pleading. "Mr. Stone, there's a strange-acting man out here around the house. He tried to get me to come out and talk to him. Something's wrong about him."

She gave a brief description of the man, a medium-built red-head she thought, and what had happened. Not knowing what else to do, she went to the living room and sat on the edge of the sofa to wait. Shivering with anxiety, she felt the minutes stretch into what seemed hours before Mr. Stone finally rang the doorbell.

Relieved to see that it was Mr. Stone, she unlocked and opened the door to talk to him, but his bored, perfunctory manner did nothing to reassure her. He listened to her, then went outside to have a look around. Earline thought his search around the property more token than useful, and she wasn't surprised when he reported finding nothing. He left.

Not long after Mr. Stone left, Earline heard scratching, scraping sounds at the east window; someone was trying to get into her bedroom. Though she was disappointed in Stone's earlier search, she didn't know of another option. There was no phone in the cabin where Bob was sleeping, and there was no one else to call. Again, she dialed Stone's number. A few minutes later, he came back and, tight-jawed, looked around, and again found nothing.

Following his departure, there came more scratching, scraping at the door. For a third time she called him, and for a third time Mr. Stone came out, looked around and found nothing. Later Earline would recall the dogs out back in their pen, barking for long periods of time. Thinking back, she wondered if maybe the man had been hiding in the branches of a pecan tree in the orchard bordering her property. Stone's search hadn't gone far, not far at all. And much later she learned that the man had, in fact, been up in a tree.

At least she'd persuaded Stone to alert Bob, oblivious there in one of his little cabins, and send him home. But before he could dress and make his way to the house, a second man, this one with light-colored hair, appeared at the front door, wiggling his fingers, trying to get Earline to come out. She was fed up. She was ready for him, whoever it was. No doubt, the man was not ready for Earline. Holding her .38 Smith & Wesson long-barrel, pearl-handled police special, she pointed it at the surprised man, and said, "Move toward the road."

Expecting Mr. Stone to drive up any minute, on his way back from alerting Bob, she marched the man as far as the ditch, which separated the front yard from the road. He stopped, just as Stone's car appeared. The man looked down at the ditch and whined, "I can't get over this ditch!"

Jamming the gun in his back, Earline said, "Oh, I think you can."

She was right. He could. And he walked right into Mr. Stone's arms. Stone searched the man and his car, again in what Earline thought a token manner. Stone, ignoring the burglary tools—crowbar, skeleton keys, screwdrivers—Earline could see on the floor of the car, asked him a few questions, wrote down his name, address, and license number, then let him go. Said he couldn't arrest a man because of some tools in his car. Just like that. Earline couldn't believe it.

Bob arrived just as Stone drove away. They sat together at the dining room table as Earline filled him in on the night's events. After

Chapter Eight: A Turning Point

they'd gone through it all, Bob pointed out that it was nearly daylight. "He won't come back. Let's get some sleep."

Bob slept soundly, but the car cruising several times up and down the normally deserted road in front of the house got Earline's attention. Unable to wind down, she gave up on sleep and went into the kitchen to make coffee. She was amazed that the six kids in the back were still asleep, although Bruce had gotten up once to see what was going on. She'd sent him back to bed, and he'd stayed there.

After putting the coffee on to percolate, Earline walked back toward the bedroom. As she passed the hallway, she saw, incredibly, a man's face staring in through the little window. He motioned for her to come out.

That did it. She ran to the bedroom, yelling to Bob that the man was back, and grabbed the gun from the dresser top where she'd left it. Darting back to the hallway, she pointed the gun at the door and pulled the trigger.

The first bullet hit the wall beside the door. The outside of that wall consisted of two layers of brick, and hitting it, the bullet ricocheted, shattering the large, round mirror on the hallway wall to Earline's left. She heard the bullet whistle past her ear, barely missing her head. Thinking it was the man shooting at her, she fired again, and again and again—four bullet holes right through her beautiful door. One found its target, although Earline didn't yet know it.

She saw him turn, as if to run. Fury propelling her, she yanked open the shot-up door and ran after him. He scampered around Bob's pick-up truck, parked in the drive next to the porch. Round and round the truck they went until she spoke, her voice steady and hard, "If you run, I'll shoot you!"

His abrupt stop and shaky wheedling voice told her he knew she would do just that. They stood facing each other, Earline holding the pistol with both hands and aiming right at him.

Bob, finally awake, came running out, barefoot, wearing only his boxer shorts. He grabbed the man by the collar and pulled his fist back to hit him. That's when he saw the blood. "Hell, Earline! You shot him!"

The man's hand lay against his heart, blood streaming down his chest. It looked as if Earline had shot him right in the heart. Seeing this, Earline's "feathers fell," as she would later describe it. She hadn't meant to kill anybody. She'd just wanted him to leave her and her kids alone.

Bob dropped his hand from the man's collar and looking at Earline, said, "Go in the house and call Captain Nichols."

Earline knew that calling Captain Nichols, head of the Apalachee Correctional Institute, located less than a mile away, made sense. But she wasn't going to do it. "I'm not going inside. You'll let him go." She knew Bob pretty well.

Knowing Earline's resolve, Bob went inside to make the call. Still holding the gun on the man, she got the feeling he was hatching a plan. She knew he was either going to come at her or run. He chose the latter. She shot at his heels but didn't hit him. She pulled the trigger again, and the pistol clicked. Empty. At the click, Earline turned and ran just as fast—in the opposite direction, back into the house.

She would say later, "All my courage left me. There was blood all over the porch because that bullet jammed in the back of his hand in the middle of all those veins. He bled like a stuck hog. I didn't see the blood when I came outside. I guess I ran right over it when I was after him. I had my eye on the prey!"

Within minutes Captain Nichols arrived. Bob had called right away to say the man had bolted, and the Captain brought several guards with their dogs. Hound dogs. Bloodhounds. According to Earline, "That was scary enough, right there, five or six dogs baying like crazy."

The dogs traced the man several miles through the woods and over to River Road, and the Marianna police picked him up there. Just as he was put into the patrol car, he passed out—alcohol and loss of blood contributing to his condition. He would remain in the hospital for many weeks, recovering from the lead poisoning that

Chapter Eight: A Turning Point

had set in. Earline wouldn't know his fate after that.

The police searched around the house, finding a quart of liquor under one window and human feces under another. Earline thought about the recent burglary at Bob's restaurant and was convinced those men had intended to rob the house.

Badly shaken by this event, Earline would never again feel safe in her beautiful house. But her reputation as a ferocious defender of her home and family spread like wildfire. Several weeks later, a different kind of incident hinted at what some people thought of Earline's daring. Friends C.G. and Hazel came home after an evening out to find a strange man asleep on their sofa. The man was buck naked. Although he didn't do it, C.G. told Hazel he wanted to call Earline to come shoot him. Later he said, "I didn't want to call Bob. He would've just let him go."

And concerning the arrival of others to her home, "Well, all I can say, after that time with the man and the gun, anybody wanted to come to my house, they'd call me from the road. They didn't walk unannounced into my yard."

But despite her now legendary bravery, the shooting marked a shift in Earline's outlook and a turning point in her life. Her fears would not be put to rest. "Even if a stick cracked in the yard, I'd go all to pieces."

She had known that Sneads was getting to be a meaner kind of place, but now the intrusion on her own home, the danger she felt for her children had become too much. Added to that was Bob's almost complete preoccupation with his entrepreneurial efforts, including the popular restaurant at which one could get a decent drink in that dry county, his cabins, real estate development, and running all the concessions at the major dam project nearby. She began to think about other places, at least as temporary havens, places that could be less dangerous.

Before long, she was back on the road, this time with her three kids and Rubye in tow.

≫•≪

CHAPTER NINE

In and Out of a Storybook

ONCE MORE, EARLINE FELT THE LURE OF TRAVEL. SHE longed to see the west again. Like a magnet, its steady pull drew her. And she wanted Rubye and her children to see it. A long trip would be fun for them all; it would be educational and offer adventure. And it would take them away from Sneads for a while. They would leave as soon as school was out for the summer.

Early June, 1953, with maps current, cooler filled, and clothes packed, Earline and her little band of travelers headed west on Highway 90, destination—Colorado. About sixty miles west of Sneads, they stopped by Jack and Mary Alice's house in DeFuniak Springs, much to the kids' delight. Earline knew, and so did they, that Mary Alice would have a stack of comic books for them. This was a mixed blessing in Earline's eyes. Superman, Wonder Woman, and Captain Marvel would be good entertainment during the long stretches of driving, cutting down on sibling bickering. But she didn't want those comics competing with the natural marvels her children could, and should, see, one big reason for making the trip.

In later years she would realize the sights had won over comic book heroes when her adult children talked about memories of the sun sinking below the horizon of the vast plains, the brown and swirling mighty Mississippi below a high bridge, or the first glimpse of the mountains nudging the skyline. Their memories echoed those of her first trip west, back in 1942, giving her double pleasure.

Leaving the Florida panhandle and the entrepreneurial Bob behind with his all-consuming work, the little band motored steadily west in the shiny red 1952 Chevy convertible with its black canvas top. After a brief stop in Metairie, Louisiana for a visit with Aunt Bunch and Uncle Jack, they were back on the road headed for high adventure.

The impish Bruce at ten, solemn Carol, eight, and the three-year-old fireball Susan, behaved relatively well on the 1,600-mile journey, all things considered. For fifteen-year-old Rubye, who was quickly developing her adolescent independence, this would be her only trip west until later in her adult life.

Each day Earline drove six to ten hours, with periodic rest stops, until she was tired, or the kids were starting to pick on each other from restlessness. Around noon, they'd stop for a picnic lunch at a wayside rest stop or some other inviting place to pull off the road to feast on canned baked beans, Vienna sausages, bologna and crackers, fruit cocktail. Earline and her little ones loved those picnics, but restaurants were a treat, as well.

Earline wanted her children to learn to be responsible, and one of those responsibilities was knowing how to behave in public. When in restaurants, she encouraged them to order for themselves. Bruce usually asked for a hamburger; Carol often chose a hot roast-beef sandwich—thinly sliced roast beef on white bread smothered with gravy, but Susan's selection never varied. "I want a cold weenie," she'd announce to the entire room in her shrill, high-pitched voice.

If the cook wasn't paying attention and the weenie happened to get heated or appear on a bun, the little dark-haired, chubby-cheeked girl would unabashedly share her reaction, much to other customers' amusement and the waitress's chagrin. By then, Earline was used to Susan's irrepressible self.

At day's end they'd look for a motel with a swimming pool, their reward at the end of their long, hot rides in those pre-air-conditioning

Chapter Nine: In and Out of a Storybook

days. Even having all the car's windows open couldn't keep the stalwart vacationers from melting as they drove by kudzu and cotton fields, across plains and prairies. Where there weren't swarms of bugs, there was dust, and sometimes both.

They spent the whole summer, glorious June, July, and August, traveling to and in Colorado. On that first trip, they went to Empire, a small village along Highway 40 on Berthod Pass's east side. Earline had first seen and fallen in love with the area twelve years earlier. She'd known, and vowed, she would return. And so she had.

In Empire, soon-to-be-friend Carole Walker related her take on meeting the Wilson travelers. She spotted their red convertible as it turned down the road to her parents' motel cabins. Earline was looking for a place to stay, and signs led her to the Walkers' cabins. Carole was looking for Rock Hudson. Working as a waitress in Empire's Hard Rock Cafe, a local eatery and meeting place much different from the international chain of today, Carole had heard that Rock was in the area—driving around in a red convertible. Seeing Earline's car turn down her drive, her hopes soared as she dashed out of the cafe and sprinted after it. Deeply disappointed that the car contained not Rock, but a young family, she nevertheless was as cordial as a crestfallen teenager could be. She and her family—brother Jesse, parents Virginia and Jesse Senior— became life-long friends of Earline and family.

The following few years, while always visiting for a while in Empire, Earline and her brood also stayed in other enchanting places. There was the sweet little cottage in Bakerville, between Silver Plume and Loveland Pass, where they all searched for gold and the kids played with a litter of kittens. At Miz Scofield's Wee-Two Ranch in the forested mountains above Nederland, their lodging was a wonderfully rustic cabin. There, the old wood stove provided homey warmth during the chilly mornings, and eccentric, reclusive Miz Scofield offered cookies or fresh gingerbread in the afternoons. She identified myriad birds in the trees and the small furry rodents skittering among the rocks as the children sat spellbound, listening young minds and happy tummies feasting on the bounty of this special place and time.

Earline and Miz Scofield would be friends for decades, until Miz Scofield's passing in the 1980s. Both women possessed fiercely independent spirits and neither hesitated to do combat in matters that concerned people and issues they cared about. Though the refuge each sought differed, Earline's in travel, and the older Miz Scofield's in her mountain haven, they shared a deep love of nature and a mutual respect for the unique individual each one was.

The trips, the movement, the new sights, the delight of it all. Earline embraced these treasured experiences. But it was being in the Colorado mountains that she loved most. Her children, too, felt an open-hearted joy and sense of freedom unlike any they'd experienced anywhere else. That's why, several summer trips after the first, she bought a two-storey, Victorian gingerbread house in Empire. Earline and her children would spend several summers in those magical, beautiful hills, then live there year-round for a storybook eighteen months. Bob, hardworking, always working Bob, would visit occasionally.

Earline made friends easily, and in Empire she had a community of friends, the likes of which she'd never experienced. Many of these lasted a lifetime. Virginia Walker was one, as was Mary MacDonald, a delightful, effervescent southern woman who lived with her husband, Mac, and her pet goose, Lucy, in a beautiful log house nestled in the mountains at Empire's western edge. Gwen, an artist who later moved to Tucson, and Pearl who had a delightful shop right there in Empire, also numbered in the friend crowd. And there was Eula Guanella, whose husband's grandparents had explored and settled the area more than a century earlier, and whose three children were about the same ages as Earline's. The Guanellas lived in the massive, rustic ancestral lodge a short distance up Highway 40.

Dr. Josephine Harris was a classically elegant woman, born in

Chapter Nine: In and Out of a Storybook

the waning years of the nineteenth century. She was a trailblazer, attending chiropractic school when women rarely did that sort of thing, and had her own successful chiropractic practice. She'd retired to Empire, filling her time with friends, reading, playing the piano and organ at home and for the little community church that sat right across Highway 40 from her house. Earline recognized echoes of her own mama in Dr. Jo, in her honesty, integrity, and warmth, and revered her all the more.

At that little community church across from Dr. Jo's, Earline met Reverend and Mrs. Atkinson. They became more of the warm, caring group of life-long friends, ones who would reach out to Earline with constancy over the years, and across the miles that often separated them.

With these friends and in this magical place, Earline looked on happily as her kids spent idyllic days wading in streams and lakes, often having contests to see who could stand the freezing water the longest. The winner, a dubious honor, would be unable to feel her or his feet for some time after. Earline, Eula, and sometimes Virginia, with kids in tow, picnicked, climbed mountains, hiked to abandoned gold mines, explored meadows and old graveyards. Young and old alike delighted in the columbine, Indian paintbrush, and countless other wildflowers, ate wild currants, and inhaled the scent of the fragrant pine bark.

Earline, always ready for a real or imaginary adventure, told the kids stories, just as her daddy had read to her and her siblings in their childhood. Virginia Walker, would-be Silver Screen star, would do her bit, too. "Did I ever tell y'all about the time I met Clark Gable and Hedy Lamarr?" she'd ask them, blue eyes twinkling.

In the fall of 1956, Earline decided to stay in Empire rather than return to Florida. By this time, Rubye had married and started a family of her own back in Florida. And with little to take her back to Sneads, Earline chose to extend their delightful months in Empire. She enrolled her three children in the local school, a one-room school that included grades first through eighth, student population of ten. Miss Martin taught everyone in the one large room.

For Earline, this was a blissful time. She lived in a beautiful spot, right in the palm of the Rockies. Her children were happy with the place, the other kids in town, and the school. She and her friends met often and celebrated each of their birthdays together. They lunched at The Pines at the fork of Highways 6 and 40, about a mile east of Empire, and at Mrs. Barrett's Ye Olde Pastie Shop, a sweet Victorian restaurant painted a shocking pink and featuring those meat pies so popular with miners of earlier days

Earline and her friends were important parts of each other's lives. Next-door neighbors, Nell and Tully Nelson, were in and out of Earline's home, as she and her kids were in and out of theirs. Tully, the postmaster, also ran a lovely old souvenir shop with his wife. Never before, and never after this time, had Earline felt herself to be such an integral part of a community. She even served a stint on the local school board.

For herself, as well as for her children, this was a storybook time. After school and in nice weather, Bruce and his sisters roamed the hills with their friends, while in the winter they had snowball fights or went sledding or ice-skating. Sometimes they built large snow forts and pummeled each other and their forts until they could hardly stand up and could definitely no longer feel their frozen fingers. Coming home, shaking off the bulky coats and hats, they went directly into the warm kitchen where Earline would have cookies or pie fresh from the oven and hot chocolate waiting for them and their friends.

Jesse Walker, impressed by Earline's domestic skills, once proclaimed, "This pie is even better than the restaurants make!" He, Bruce, Eddie Guanella and another friend, Steve Sumner, were inseparable, and Jesse was always eager to sample Earline's baking.

School captured the three young Wilsons' attention, and for that Earline was glad and grateful. They told her about each day's

Chapter Nine: In and Out of a Storybook

highlights, what Miss Martin'd read aloud to them that day. They were all, from Susan in second grade to Bruce in eighth, captivated by tales from Rudyard Kipling's *Jungle Book*, and that wonderful mongoose Rikki Tikki Tavi in his fight with Nag, the big black cobra. She looked on with approval as they learned to play chess, practicing with each other at home, all becoming fairly proficient at it.

In the fall, Miss Martin took the students on field trips, and they were just as the name implies. Taking sack lunches, the students and their teacher walked the short distance through town and up an old mining road deeper into the forested mountains. There they collected various kinds of specimens—one day, mosses and lichen, golden aspen leaves; another day, arrays of quartz, and iron pyrite—fool's gold. Earline heard about how later, back at school, they stored their treasures until they could be investigated thoroughly, mining the leaf or rock for all kinds of information. They pressed the leaves, then later dipped them in wax for preserving.

Earline would long remember Bruce's account of Jesse's antics, which would become a part of the family's oral archives. With an impish gleam in his eye, Jess asked, "Miss Martin. How many of these leaves do you want us to mash?"

"Jesse, we are not mashing the leaves. We are pressing them."

"But how many do you want mashed?

"That depends upon what you have. But, regardless, you may write one hundred times, 'I will not mash the leaves. I will press them."

Jesse proceeded with his penance, pencil pressed to the paper with great force. After he'd finished all one hundred repetitions, he leaned across his desk and whispered to Bruce, "Miss Martin must not be very good at mashing leaves."

For Bruce, being in Empire was like being in heaven. When he wasn't in school, or at home eating or sleeping, Earline knew he and his friends were exploring the wilds around that little mountain village. Fishing in Bard Creek or nearby beaver dams, hunting, hiking and camping at remote Lake Ethel made for happy boys. But Bruce's favorite fishing was with Eddie Guanella on his family's private land where long stretches of Clear Creek housed fishing holes teeming with trout. And because the land was privately owned, no one else could be there.

As far as Bruce was concerned, being outdoors in secluded and wild places was the best thing possible. This preference was to be one of a lifetime. In his early thirties, Bruce and his wife, Sue, would move to the remote Alaskan Interior, securing one of the last homesteads in that state.

On many a Sunday afternoon Earline was delighted to find Carol having tea and a visit at Miss Martin's little cottage next to the Hard Rock cafe. Much later in life Carol would tell Earline that those visits, combined with the sheer joy and adventure that each day at school brought, led her ultimately to spend more than thirty-five years as an educator. She claimed it was Miss Martin's approach and her genius as a teacher that gave her a taste of what schooling could be. She would spend her professional life promoting the idea of building on students' natural curiosity and taking advantage of the learning opportunities that surround us everywhere.

Watching Susan make friends and take care of the Hotel Splendide's burro proved another of Earline's joys during their time in Empire. The hotel, in later years renamed The Peck House, was Colorado's oldest. It sat a city block's length behind Earline's house and had recently been restored by Velma Harrison and her sisters, granddaughters of Adolph Coors, who founded the Coors Brewing Company, and railroad pioneer Harry Colbran. Mrs. Harrison, a crusader for humane treatment of wild horses and other animals, made the hotel pet-friendly and also kept her burro, Ponce de Leone, there. Susan fell in love with the burro and became its official caretaker. Earline laughed as she watched Susan, Carol and friends lead Leone off on picnics, sharing riding time with each other. Leone and Mrs. Harrison made a permanent impression on young Susan, and Earline would attribute her daughter's time with Leone as the cause

Chapter Nine: In and Out of a Storybook

of her lasting enchantment with burros and donkeys.

A year and a half of storybook bliss. But for Earline, there was always another place to see, more travel to be had. Despite her contentment with her friends and her happiness in the community, she decided to spend the rest of the winter of 1958 in south Florida, to have a winter's vacation. Her sister Betty, who was living there, had invited Earline and family to join her and her husband, Al. Pulled by that invitation and her interest in spending the cold winter months in balmy Miami, Earline packed up her kids and headed back to Florida. She didn't know then that a return to Empire would be farther away and more short-lived than anticipated, that life had more challenging changes in store for her. Stopping by Sneads to pick up Bob, the family drove on down to Hialeah.

Chapter Ten

Another Try in Florida

Being back in Florida was one thing, but being in the Miami area was another. Southern Florida was a different Florida than she'd grown up in, and Earline thought it was lovely. She appreciated the milder winter weather and the lushness of the landscape, the palms, brilliant flowers and other tropical foliage. Being near her sister Betty brought some good times, too. They were both great practical jokers—taking unexpected pictures of the other one in the bathtub or putting some surprise in each other's food—and were gleeful when pulling one over on each other, Al, Bob or the kids. It was fun to be with Betty in a time and place where they could enjoy each other.

With her kids in school and Bob taking care of meals and other matters at home, Earline, for the first time in her married life, went to work. Not because she needed to, for Bob had put enough money aside to tide them over during this interlude, but because she wanted to. She'd seen a newspaper ad for a job with an insurance company, canvassing, getting leads in neighborhoods in Hialeah and nearby communities. Given her carnival experience, working for Uncle John, and then with Roy Green, she felt at ease meeting new people, initiating conversation, especially if it meant a potential sale. That was like winning a prize. The job offered a challenge, one that intrigued Earline.

Passing the insurance test posed the first hurdle. Earline browbeat Betty into taking the test, too, with the idea they would work together. Earline studied for weeks, and when test time came, she scored 90 per cent. Reluctant Betty read through the material twice and scored 100.

Their job involved making contacts and building interest in the company's insurance policies, getting a certain number of potential clients in order to meet their weekly quotas. The two sisters, pretty, personable and sharp as tacks, had no problem in meeting quotas, often getting "multiples," or multiple quotas, in a single day.

Since their interest in having fun equaled that of doing well on the job, when they exceeded their quotas for the day, they'd hold some of the names back and submit them the next day. And then they'd go fishing, which they loved, whether just the two of them or with spouses and kids.

Fishing figured largely in those southern Florida months, and not only for Earline and Betty's weekday trips. Weekends, Earline, Bob, Betty, Al, Bruce, Carol, and Susan sometimes headed down to Key West, but most often out on the untamed Tamiami Trail. Some said that name came from a contraction—"Tampa to Miami Trail," referring to the paved road across the wild Everglades. But Earline and her sister didn't care much about the name; it was the fishing, picnicking, and occasional camping there they loved.

For one overnight camping trip, they found a small park next to a lake deep in the Everglades. Earline and Bob walked around the spot, admiring the tall cypresses, trunks rising from the gray-green swampy water to support long branches dripping with Spanish moss. Tropical birds sat on tree limbs or floated on the water—delicate snowy egrets; non-water-proof-anhingas, sometimes called snake birds or water turkeys because of their long necks, perching on stumps, lifting their broad wings out to dry; moorhens with their black heads and necks and surprising red bills. Turtles lined up on fallen trees or stuck their heads out of the water. Every now and

Chapter Ten: Another Try in Florida

then, they'd hear a rustle in the bushes suggesting the slither of a snake. The jungle, lush green plants and teeming life, crowded the land, making the blacktop parking area seem a good place for the campers to settle.

As they began unpacking a few things from the car, Earline suggested they might look around for alligators. It was the Everglades, after all. Minutes later, Betty called out that she'd spotted one and soon Earline, kids, and Al all crowded around.

Betty yelled to Bob as she and the kids stood by the water's edge feeding that alligator the bacon they'd brought for their breakfast. "Come over here, Bob. You have to see this cute little thing."

Dropping the blankets he'd just taken out of the car, having decided on the fairly level spot where he figured he'd sleep, Bob went over for a look. He took one look at the young, three-foot gator and, without a word to anyone, walked back, picked up his blankets, and put them in the station wagon. That glimpse of the alligator was all it took to change his mind about sleeping outside.

His decision created a predicament. The three kids were to sleep in the car. Earline had planned to sleep in the car. Now, Bob, a vigorous snorer, would be in there with them. Knowing she couldn't take that snoring in such close quarters, Earline asked Betty and Al if she could sleep in their car with them. Of course, they agreed.

Blanket in hand, she crawled into the back of their station wagon, snuggled the blanket around her, and settled in. But soon she was wiggling, waking the others.

"What's going on?" Al asked.

"It feels like something's crawling on me."

"Oh, shut up and go to sleep, Earline. It's just those old palmetto bugs. They're all over the car."

Palmetto bugs. A nicer name for cockroaches. Earline despised roaches. But the choice was roaches, jungle critters on the night prowl, or Bob's snoring. She chose roaches.

≫•≪

With the school semester over and the weather growing warmer, Earline and Bob packed up and took the family back to Sneads, where Bob would stay, getting back to work. But Earline and the kids stopped only long enough to re-supply before heading back to Colorado, to Empire, for the summer. This time, though, it was only for the summer. Earline had agreed to return to Sneads for the school year. She'd return to their beautiful home, the one that no longer felt so safe to her. She'd be back in the place where she'd grown up, back to volunteering at the school, back to fewer opportunities to expand her world and her children's.

While Earline and the kids were in Colorado for the summer, Bob began work on a new project. This was a small store, in which he would sell snacks, sandwiches, and beverages. It was also a service station. The store sat at the northeast corner of the successful BruCaSue Subdivision, which he, with Earline's support, had developed some five years earlier. And it was just a mile from Lake Seminole.

In addition to having the store, Bob helped oversee trusties from the nearby Apalachee Correctional Institution, the same prison from which they'd called Captain Nichols with the dogs, some six years earlier, to track the man Earline shot.

Since that time, the Corps of Engineers had completed the Jim Woodruff Dam, so Bob's concessions for that project ended. He and Earline would long remember how he'd been honored by the ceremonial pouring of the first load of concrete for that dam. But its completion in the past year, 1957, meant the end of that demanding business, making it possible for Bob to join the family for the early 1958 south Florida jaunt.

But now another phase of work had begun, which included cleaning up the brush and forest undergrowth for Three Rivers State Park. The park was one of several to be created on the shores of Lake Seminole, the huge, beautiful lake coming out of the damming of three rivers—the Chattahoochee, Flint, and Apalachicola. Lake Seminole now covered 37,500 acres of water with 18,000 acres of

Chapter Ten: Another Try in Florida

surrounding land, lying where Georgia and Florida met. From the beginning, the lake created a big asset for nearby towns, including Sneads.

Bob, whose general interest in contributing to the community led him to oversee the work of trusties at the nearby Three Rivers State Park, was supervising some brush-clearing. Always generous, despite the prison guards' warnings, he was known to give cigarettes to these prisoner trusties.

On one late winter's day, Bob was burning leaves, a chore he loved doing. As he tended the fire, one of the prisoners approached him and asked for a cigarette. Obligingly, he dug into his shirt pocket and pulled one out. As he reached to hand off the cigarette, a second prisoner slipped up behind him, ax raised and aimed at Bob's head. The blade came down, its force knocking Bob to his knees and then into the fire. Out cold, he lay in the flames till a nearby guard who'd witnessed what happened was able to rush over and pull him out.

The two prisoners, along with three others, scrambled into Bob's truck, his trademark 1955 black Chevrolet pick-up, knowing they'd find the keys in the ignition. In seconds they had the truck tearing through the brush, down the road, heading for highway 90 and freedom. Or so they thought.

With no inkling of what had happened, Earline, who was tending the store, heard the truck coming down the road. Some fifty-two years later she recalled, "I mean, it was mortally flying! They knew I'd be in the store, and four of them lay down on the floor so I thought there was just one in the truck. I knew it was Bob's truck, and I knew something bad must have happened."

Earline soon found out just how bad that something was. She saw two guards taking Bob from a car into a house nearby. She bolted the hundred yards to the house, leaving the gas pumps, cash register, and store unlocked. The first thing she saw as she entered was Bob walking around, dazed, his face white as a sheet, except for the blood. Blood was pouring from his head, over his face, down his neck, over his shirt. Everywhere. To a horrified Earline, her husband looked like a dead man walking.

With the closest hospital more than twenty-five miles away and the family doctor—the nearest doctor, Jimmy Thompson, in Chattahoochee—within five miles, the thing to do was obvious. The guards wrapped Bob's head in towels and put him in Earline's car. She drove as fast as she could down Highway 90, across the river, and up the hill into Chattahoochee.

At Jimmy Thompson's office, knowing she couldn't get Bob out of the car by herself, she ran in to get help. Jimmy took one look into her pale, stricken face, and saw her lips moving, making no sound. "I think something's happened to one of the kids. Go with her and see," he said to Elsie, his wife and assistant.

On the way out they met a man who had seen Bob in the car and was bringing him in. Jimmy looked at Bob, then at Earline. Try as she did, she still couldn't get words to come out of her mouth. She didn't begin to calm down till Jimmy gave her a shot. He'd then stitched Bob's head the best he could and told Earline to take him to the hospital in Quincy, another twenty miles to the east. Earline was grateful the doctors kept Bob in the hospital for several days to make sure he was all right before letting him go home.

The attack and its aftermath were both horrifying and terrifying to Earline. She was used to running Bob across the bridge to the doctor the several times he'd cut his arm on broken glass at his restaurant, or for the recurring bee stings to which he had intense reactions. But this situation held a sense of violence and vulnerability that echoed the shooting six years ago. It foreshadowed a change in Bob, a dark one; he would not return to his consistent good humor. From then on, it was rare for him to laugh and demonstrate the Ringling Brothers' chicken walk, balance a chair on his nose, or come up with the puns that delighted everyone. His good humor wouldn't disappear completely, but receded. And over time, his nervousness and irritability increased.

Chapter Ten: Another Try in Florida

The prisoners were tracked and caught. The truck was spotted outside a church in Alabama where the escapees were hiding. That was also where they were arrested and badly beaten, then thrown back into prison. Reportedly, their cell consisted of nothing more than bars and a concrete floor. No bed. No covers. Nothing. One had been in for murder but was up for parole. The others, too, but it was a long, long time before any of them saw the outside of a prison again.

Earline went on as best she could, but she was unhappy. Bob still didn't want to leave, and after a year of trying to make it work, several months after the prisoners' attack, she packed up again. At the end of the school term she and the kids went west again. This time it was back to Empire, to community, to revitalizing friendships, and to the reassurance of those majestic mountains.

CHAPTER ELEVEN

Challenges at High Altitude

RELIEVED AND HAPPY TO BE BACK IN THE FRESH MOUNTAIN air and peaceful surroundings, Earline joyfully renewed her Colorado friendships. As she easily fell back in with Virginia, Eula, Mary, Pearl, Dr. Jo, and her many other friends in Empire, she watched with delight as her kids romped with their friends, Leone the burro among them. And by the end of summer, Bob decided to join his family. The Florida home sold, he closed his business, packed up his black Chevrolet pick-up and drove out to Colorado.

In Empire, Earline knew the sweet Victorian house she'd bought several years earlier needed attention, beginning with the old shed behind the house—that decrepit structure had to go. Bob wanted a project and set to work to take it down, although Earline was concerned about him doing such heavy work. His recent visit to the doctor had revealed weakness in his heart, as well as late-onset diabetes. But he was determined to take on that shed.

The children had just begun the school year. Because Clear Creek County had consolidated its schools, closing the one in Empire, the fall of 1959 found Bruce, a high-school junior, and Carol, a sophomore, riding the school bus to Idaho Springs High School, nine miles down the highway. Susan, now a fifth grader, traveled to Georgetown, about five miles away.

On a lovely September Saturday, Bob was working on the shed, and Earline was busy in the dining room. She heard him come through the back door and turned to see him staggering toward her, his face grey and his eyes dimmed by pain. She knew she needed to act fast. She managed to support him to the bed, where he collapsed. Scarcely able to breathe herself, she reached for the phone to call the doctor in Idaho Springs and shouted at nine-year-old Susan to go get her brother and sister. Earline and Susan both knew they were with Jesse scouting at the dump on the east end of town. Wide-eyed and pale, Susan took off running.

Not long after, all running the half-mile from the dump back to the house, the children heard the sirens scream past, headed for their house and their dad.

The doctor arrived just nine minutes after Earline had called, and she was relieved that he'd also contacted the highway patrol, who followed him, bringing oxygen. Still rattled when the ambulance came with its efficient and competent emergency technicians, Earline watched with greater relief and gratitude as the doctor and the technicians did their work. They lifted Bob to a stretcher, took him through the house and across the yard toward the ambulance's open back door, moving with cautious speed and skill.

With Bob safely inside and the doctor by his side to make sure he had oxygen on the trip, the ambulance pulled away, and Earline and the kids piled into their car. Their own hearts in their throats, they followed the ambulance down the hill, past Idaho Springs, and the long forty miles to Denver's St. Joseph's Hospital.

Emergency treatment and further examinations from the hospital's medical team revealed that, just as Earline suspected and feared, Bob had suffered a major heart attack. Throughout his six-week stay at St. Joe's, his condition was touch-and-go for too many of those weeks. The ambiguity of his prognosis was terrifying to Earline and her children. Those days and nights brought not only uncertainty about whether Bob would survive, but also dark questions about what his illness portended for their family. Earline was sure of one

Chapter Eleven: Challenges at High Altitude

thing— life wouldn't be the same.

In that last, Earline was certainly correct. Bob's heart attack and its consequences did indeed usher in big changes for the family. After having finally made the decision to live in Empire and then the move itself, she now found it was no longer possible to stay in the place they so loved Empire's elevation of 8,614 feet was too high for Bob in his condition, the air too thin with too little oxygen for his weak heart. The family would have to move.

Looking at the possibilities, Earline soon determined that Golden, a small town west of Denver at the base of the foothills, would be their new home. It was as close to the mountains as she could get and, with an elevation of 5,674, it was nearly 3,000 feet lower than Empire. Golden also had a reputation for good schools. Only weeks after Bob's heart attack, Earline sold the beloved Empire home, bought one in Golden, and enrolled her children in school.

Further amplifying change, Earline became the family's wage-earner. Bob needed recovery time, and even when he did improve enough, Earline wasn't convinced he'd be able to work. She didn't know what kind of work his condition, let alone his temperament, would allow, or what opportunities might be available. But she did know the family had to be supported, and she would need a job. The storybook life of Empire was over for good.

Earline found a factory job at Coors Porcelain Company; Susan, Carol, and Bruce attended school; and Bob stayed home. He prepared meals and did what he could to help out around the house. Even at the lower altitude, though, weakness and shortness of breath limited his activities for some time.

≫•≪

DURING THE GOLDEN YEARS, WHICH OFTEN DIDN'T SEEM ALL that golden to Earline, she and Bob tried their best to create a good home for themselves and their children. The challenges were many, with Earline first working at the porcelain company, often on night shift, and Bob being mostly homebound and fretting from lack of activity. But his health gradually improved, and Earline found other jobs that better suited her and the situation, first with an insurance company.

In the coming years, Earline would meet many people through her work, and some would become life-long friends. Little Peggy Chavez was one. It was while she was on an in-home sales visit that she met Peggy, a little girl with dark hair and big brown eyes. Earline felt an instant connection with that little tot, a connection that would see them both through many of life's challenges and changes. Friendship was in the cards for Earline and Mrs. Chavez, Peggy's mother, too. Earline saw the family as often as she could when she worked in that neighborhood. But that insurance sales job ended after a man tried to accost her one night. With regret, she realized the neighborhoods assigned to her had become more dangerous, too dangerous for a single woman going door-to-door. Even after she'd moved on to another job, she still called or visited Peggy and her family when she could.

Taking a job selling sewing machines at J.C. Penny's in nearby Lakewood seemed a natural next step. One day after several months on the job, on what seemed like a normal workday, the store manager asked her to come to his office. On her way there, she couldn't help but wonder why she'd been called in—was there some new store policy she'd missed? Did he want her to do something differently? As she entered, the manager looked up from his desk, beaming, holding a letter, which he waved as he greeted her.

"Congratulations," he said, grinning from ear to ear.

"For what?" Earline was more than puzzled. She had no idea what he was talking about.

"You put this store on the map. Because of you we sold more sewing machines than any other J.C. Penney in the country. A Chicago store came in second."

Earline knew she loved sales, and she knew she was good at it. But having this confirmation and recognition gave her an extra boost

Chapter Eleven: Challenges at High Altitude

and, ironically, that extra boost would lead her away from Penney's. Soon after, she was invited to work for Singer Sewing Machine Company at the May D & F Department Store in the Westland Shopping Center. The Center had opened in 1960, just a few years earlier. Earline, the natural-born salesperson did well there, too, and despite standing long hours on hard floors, she enjoyed her job.

Never one to be satisfied with the status quo, Earline was always on the look-out for expertise to add to her repertoire. A perfect opportunity came along one day at the downtown Denver May D&F, where she saw a young woman monogramming towels. Intrigued, Earline set out to find out more about that craft, and the more she learned, the more she wanted to do it. Ultimately, Bob helped her buy a commercial monogramming machine, and she put herself to work learning how to use it. An experimenter preferring to learn through trial and error, Earline taught herself. Then, while still with Singer, she was also hired to do monogramming, taking the orders home to do them there.

During this period, she learned about alternations, too, but monogramming was her priority. When Singer moved all of its operations to a downtown center, Earline was there with her monogramming machine to produce orders on the spot for customers. She enjoyed creating those lovely letters, but eventually, when her eyes began to suffer from the close work under poor lighting, she had to let it go.

At one point, Earline decided to learn office skills, thinking that might open up some job opportunities, and she could work better hours and with fewer demands on her physical self. She enrolled in Parks Business School. There, in January of 1961, she met June Lease, a young woman who sat behind Earline in typing class. They both were having a little trouble typing without looking at the typewriter, but they managed to do all right. Earline thought June the better typist. The two became fast friends in a friendship that would last a lifetime.

As for the office skills, Earline did find a job in an insurance company, working for a man named Hendricks and others in the office. She could write letters, but all the filing, notetaking, and other secretarial tasks flummoxed her. "Why Hendricks hired me, I'll never know. But it made me know I didn't want to do that kind of work," she would later say. "I didn't like office work—too confining, everyday doing the same thing. I liked Hendricks and the guys who worked for him, but he sure had to have patience."

CREATIVE EARLINE DIDN'T CONFINE HER ENERGY AND EFFORTS to the workplace. She also set them loose at home. They'd made that 1959 move into a newly-built ranch-style house that came with an undeveloped yard. Over next few years, out of that space of bare dirt and rock, she and Bob created a colorful high-plains oasis, with terraced flower beds, shrubs, and trees, complete with a beautiful flagstone patio, which Bob built after he'd regained some strength. Earline's knack with plants ensured that her family's nest was again surrounded by beauty.

Within two years of the move, however, the nest would begin emptying. Earline could hardly believe that, in 1961, Bruce was graduating from high school. It felt strange to her when he left to spend the summer working for the United States Geologic Survey in Wyoming. Not long after getting there, he suffered an appendectomy, and she and Bob rushed up to the Rawlins hospital to see him. Now, Bob wasn't good at hospitals. He'd been a reluctant visitor when Earline had delivered each of the kids, as well as when she'd had kidney surgery years before. That day, arriving at Bruce's room, all it took was one look at his pale, young son lying in bed, and Bob's knees folded. He sank to the floor, causing quite the stir. The hospital staff insisted on keeping him for observation to make sure he didn't have another heart attack.

In the meantime, Earline returned to Golden to check on Susan and Carol, then drove back to Rawlins about a week later to bring

Chapter Eleven: Challenges at High Altitude 111

Bob and Bruce back home. After a brief convalescence, it was back to Wyoming for Bruce. Not long after his return and right at the end of his stint with the USGS, he read a book on French foot boxing and was trying out a move, when he broke his leg. Back home with nothing to do but mend his leg, he hung around the house and saw his friends.

Earline and Bob had no idea that Bruce was toying with the idea of joining the Marine Corps. Though he didn't have a job, wasn't really looking for one, he still wasn't quite ready to take that big step of signing up. Then, Bob gave Bruce the nudge he needed. Still not able to hold a full-time job himself and mostly at home, Bob was tired of his grown son hanging around the house day after day.

"You have to find a job," Bob told him in frustration. "If you plan on coming home tomorrow, you'd better have one."

The next day Bruce joined the Marine Corps.

Earline, surprised by the step Bruce had taken, could nonetheless acknowledge her son's enthusiasm for the military, and especially for the rugged Marine Corps. Seeing him off again, she kept track of his progress. She learned that after basic training in San Diego's Camp Pendleton, a major training center for new recruits and for amphibious warfare, Bruce's supervising officer assigned him several desk jobs. Bruce detested those jobs, and Earline couldn't imagine her son at a desk all day. The one and only time he'd enjoyed being at one was in elementary school when he'd slipped into the classroom one Monday morning a few minutes before the teacher came in. Yawning, stretching and blinking, he looked right at the startled young woman, and said, "Hey, Miss Grace! Gosh, I've been in here all weekend."

At Camp Pendleton Bruce made several unsuccessful attempts to find something he wanted to specialize in. He ended up in amphibious tractors, but then heard of an opportunity with a guard attachment in Newfoundland. He'd heard of Newfoundland but that was about it. But it was far away, and far-away places seemed to call her son as much as they called Earline. He read all he could find about it and then spent the next year and a half experiencing it first-hand.

Another milestone came in 1962, when Carol graduated from high school. For several years, Earline had encouraged her oldest daughter to attend college, which would be a first in their family. When she did, Earline sold the piano to pay her tuition. Although Carol didn't go far, to the university in Boulder a mere twenty-five miles away, with Bruce off in distant lands, Earline's nest was feeling pretty deserted.

Then early in 1964, the end came for Earline's and Bob's marriage. The tensions and frictions that had been eating away at their relationship for years erupted into a final, shattering argument. The one point of agreement between them was that it was over. Bob packed his truck and returned to Sneads; Earline and Susan stayed on in Golden. A few months later, in June, 1964, after twenty-five years together, the marriage officially ended.

LIFE AFTER THE SEPARATION AND DIVORCE WOULD BRING some good times, as well as more challenges for Earline. Among the good was her decision to take dance classes at the American School of Dance. With little extra money for the fees, but determination on her side, she borrowed one hundred dollars from the local bank. But when she went downtown to the studio to sign up, she learned the price of the lessons was more than four hundred dollars. "Can I just take one-hundred dollars worth of lessons?" she asked.

"We don't do it that way," the man told her.

"Well, I guess I can't do it then, because one hundred is all I have."

"Okay. You come on down, and we'll do something for you."

She went and stayed for the first lesson, and the next, and the next. She was a hit with dance instructors and other clients, alike, and the studio people kept asking her to return. Their practice was to take a photo of each client with an instructor, but they went further with Earline—they put her photo in the window of the downtown studio. Later she would reminisce, "I guess they liked my looks and

Chapter Eleven: Challenges at High Altitude

my character. They had to have a lot of patience, because I have two left feet."

It was only when Earline's job required her to work nights that she gave up her Thursday night dancing lessons. But she remembered all she'd learned at the studio about how to follow the lead whatever the dance was. A singular experience in Earline's life.

AS FOR THE CHALLENGES, ALTHOUGH SHE WOULD LATER FIND the dates blurred by the decades, Earline would remember working at Rocky Mountain Orthodontics, a Denver company specializing in prefabricated orthodontic appliances. Routine in nature and paying as well as any other, the job provided enough income for the moment, and the moment was all Earline could handle. The job also allowed her to be home with teenaged Susan in the evenings.

It was at Rocky Mountain Orthodontics that she encountered Betty, a young woman who came to Denver through her random travels with her two children and a woman friend. Betty and that friend worked only a short while at the orthodontics company, but that was time enough for Earline to glimpse their situation and take pity on them.

The women and children were without a home, trying to survive in depressed circumstances. Earline let them stay with her and Susan for a couple of nights before the Salvation Army took them in, fed them and took care of the two children, Janice, twelve years old, and Chuck, eight, while Betty was at work.

Earline could see that Betty was struggling and that she was doing the best she could without help from her ex-husband in California, the children's father. And Earline would soon see that Betty was more than struggling; she was desperate. She told Earline her last resort was to try again for help from her ex-husband. She thought it was the only way she could afford to rent a place and settle down with the kids. Over the years, the details would fade, but Earline would never forget what happened.

Frantic Betty begged Earline to take care of Janice and Chuck for a week. "No more than a week," she promised.

She said she couldn't take them with her because she was afraid her ex-husband would take them away from her. Earline, not wanting to, but being deeply concerned for Betty and the kids, agreed. Betty pressed further for a promise from Earline—no matter what, Earline would not call Welfare Services. Again Earline agreed, and Betty and her friend left for California.

Several days passed. Then a week and still no word. Earline tried phoning Betty and left messages for her. Finally, a couple of weeks later, Betty called. She assured Earline that she'd be back, she'd get the money and come back. "Please, please, please don't go to Welfare," Betty begged.

Earline was in a bind. The children had no papers from any previous school, so she couldn't enroll them in school, although she tried. Unfortunately, they stayed home all day while Earline was at work and Susan was in school. Soon the neighbors were complaining. Chuck, with time on his hands and no supervision, was up to no good—spraying the neighbors' homes with the hose, running up and down the street, making noise, generally causing havoc. And she'd promised Betty she wouldn't call Welfare for help.

It was when Earline herself was feeling most desperate that the call from California came. Over time, she forgot the caller's name, but she would never forget the message. Betty had been found with a bullet in her head. With her desperation grown to the point of no return, she'd shot herself.

Shocked, stunned, and without resources, Earline found she had no alternative. Other than feeding them, she couldn't afford to buy clothes or anything else for the children. The school wouldn't take them without papers, and the children needed more attention and support than she could provide. She had no choice but to go to Welfare. At that point, things began to move. Social Services gave Earline an allowance to buy clothes and other things the kids needed.

She remembered how proud they were of those clothes. "I don't think they'd had new ones in a long, long time," she later mused.

As for the father, "The Welfare people got in touch with him pretty darn quick, and he was out there and with his new wife. I could tell they weren't too happy over the situation and having to take those kids back."

But they weren't given a choice, and before they could take them out of the state, they had to go before a judge. In court, the judge asked Janice if she wanted to go back with her father. Her twelve-year-old voice came out small and flat. "Well, I guess so."

When Chuck's turn came, he said, "I guess so, but Earline, give me your phone number because I might need to call you. Just in case!"

The court, however, couldn't allow Earline to do that, determining that a clean break would be better. One of the judges, though, did acknowledge Earline's role. "Mrs. Wilson, you're the only one who's acted with a grain of sense here," he said.

Altogether, the situation had consumed five or six weeks. Earline felt she'd done all she could in a difficult situation that couldn't have a happy outcome. But she was glad the children could be with their father, given all that had happened. She only hoped he would treat them well.

The home in Golden, one that circumstances had driven her to buy through the selling of the Empire home, had seen many ups and downs in the five years the family had been there. Now circumstances were forcing Earline to make another hard decision. Feeling her financial back against the wall, Earline put the house with its beautiful yard on the market and prepared to find a smaller, less expensive place in which she and Susan could live. What Earline couldn't know was that selling that house signaled the end of one mercurial and unsettling era and the beginning of yet another.

≫•≪

*Rubye, Earline, Santa, Carol, Bob and Bruce, December 1948.
Photographer unknown*

Bruce, Bob, Carol circa 1948. Photo by Earline

Uncle Lon Hicks, circa 1942. Photo by Earline

Margaret & Red Hicks, Aunt Bunch & Uncle Jack Morris, Mary Alice (sitting), Lou Ida Hicks (sitting), Susan, Bob (kneeling), J.W. Hicks, circa 1952. Photo by Earline.

Bruce before his piano recital, 1954.
Photo by Earline.

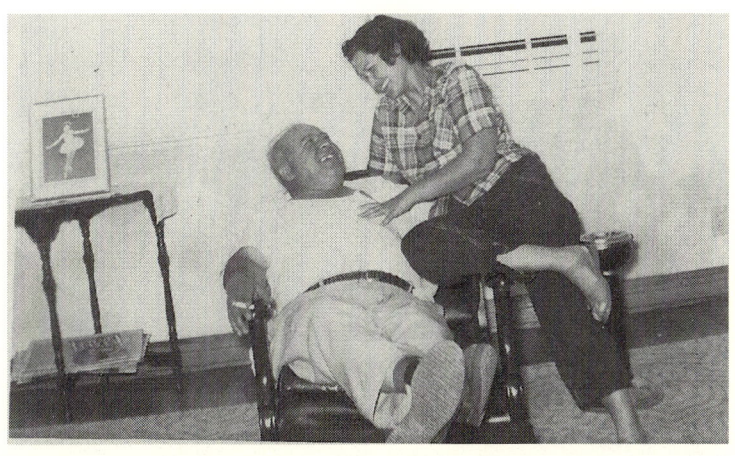

Bob & Earline, circa 1955. Photographer unknown

Susan & Carol, before a dance recital, wearing Earline's creations, circa 1955. Photo by Earline.

Susan & family pet Duchess, by the house Earline designed, circa 1955. Photo by Earline

Susan on Leone, the Hotel Splendide donkey. Empire, Colorado, circa 1956. Photo by Earline

Empire "Storybook" House, 1956. Photo by Earline

Earline, at the American School of Dance, 1964. Photo courtesy of Earline

*Earline on a hot day in front of Wilson's Cafe, Sneads, 1974.
Photo by Peggy Chavez*

*Bruce, Susan, Earline, Carol, December, 1976, Broomfield, Colorado.
Photo by Mike Pierson*

*Miz Scofield, Wee-Two Ranch, Colorado, circa 1980.
Photo by Earline*

*Earline holding Zak at Bruce & Friends' Gold Mine, Alaska, 1982.
Photo by Suzanne Wilson*

Earline with her grandchildren. Zak (left), Shari, and Rick (right), Shari's fourteenth birthday, 1984. Photo by author

The Wilson House, Florence, Colorado, 1995. Photo by Earline

The Wilson House, Florence, Colorado, 1995. Photo by Earline

Princess, 1996. Photo by Earline

Princess, 1996. Photo by Earline

Earline with sisters Rubye & Betty, Sneads, 1998. Photo by author

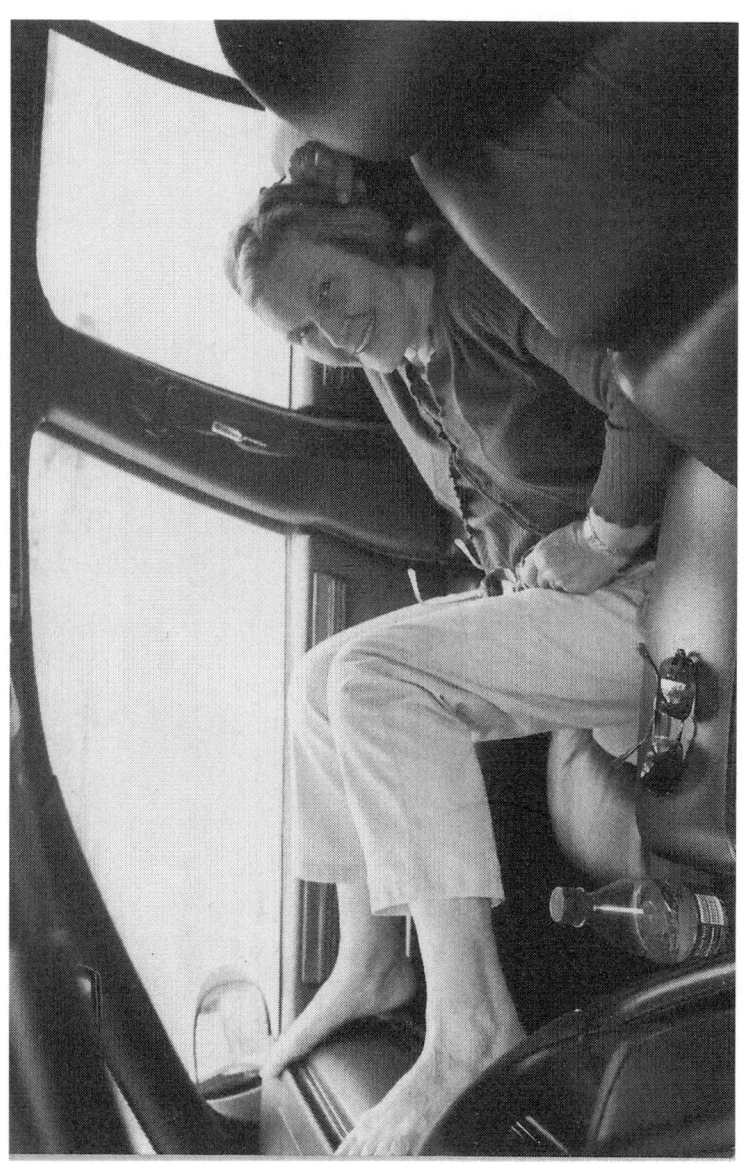

Earline, 2002, two years after the heart attack. Photo by author

Benjamin relaxing with Earline, 2005. Photo by author

First meeting of Earline & Josie: Battle of the Wills. Pace, Florida, 2007. Photo by author

Jack, Earline and Rubye, DeFuniak Springs, Florida, 2009. Photo by author

*Earline, after joining the church, October, 2010.
Photo by author*

Mystery photo!

Chapter Twelve

A Mexican Interlude

The house sold. It would be years before Earline would know that her sense of a home had been sold, too. After that, apartment living, while convenient, just wouldn't offer the feeling of home that she so loved. Nor did she yet know that she'd be living in apartments for more years than she'd care to.

At that time, she simply had no choice. She and Susan moved to a roomy apartment in Wheat Ridge, some ten miles east. The transition, difficult as it was, at least offered an opportunity for a much-needed break. Susan had finished junior high school, and Earline could take a couple weeks vacation from her monogramming work at May D&F. Memories of conversations with Bob about going to Mexico to escape the cold winters fed her desires to get away; she'd also heard it to be an inexpensive place. So, although it wasn't winter and she had Bob had parted ways, Earline and Susan took off for exotic, enticing Mexico.

Earline and Susan, mother and daughter, were in some ways two peas in a pod. Earline was now in her early forties and Susan in her early teens, but both had the same dark hair, blue eyes, and fine facial features. Mother and daughter, the pair were both kind, warm—and willful. Both were feisty, funny, unpredictable, and both were off-the-chart adventurous. But where Earline's approach to life seemed based on the kind of certainty that comes not only from experience, but as a part of who she was, Susan, even at that early age, tolerated and even welcomed ambiguity. Unlike Earline, she felt at ease with contradictory information.

They headed for Monterrey, Mexico, some thirteen hundred miles south of Denver. Earline always loved driving long distances, especially to new places, and this trip was no exception. Motoring south through Colorado and long stretches of Texas, they arrived in Monterrey, delighting in the trip so far, and eager for more. They took in some of the sights, but they were keen on seeing more of the country's interior, and then its west coast.

Earline was adventurous but not foolish. She realized that traveling in a foreign country called for some know-how she didn't yet have and thought it best to have someone with them who knew the territory. Through a tourist center she found a reputable man who could drive them part of the way to Mazatlan, their ultimate destination.

That man, whose name has been lost with time, drove them to Torreón, more than half-a-day's trip from Monterrey. By the time they arrived in Torreón, Earline was feeling confident enough to continue on her own, so their guide took a bus back to Monterey.

Full of a market town's bustle, Torreón's streets sported chickens, ducks, children, whole families, and individuals thronging the dusty streets. Haze from unidentified smoke and dust in the air masked the red stoplight. Earline, distracted by the commotion in the streets and the murky air drove right on through, though at a cautious pace.

A policeman, however, saw her run the red light and signaled her to stop. Alarmed, she did. He approached the driver's window, speaking to her in Spanish. She looked at him blankly, and he tried again. She consulted with Susan, who had taken some Spanish in school but now was quickly realizing that school Spanish and functional, conversational Spanish were two different things. The patient policeman tried a third time. Earline spoke to him in English, and it was his turn to look back blankly. No comprende. Finally, he shrugged and, drawing on what was probably his total English vocabulary said,

"Okay," and waved her on her way.

They found a room for the night and the next day continued westward. They drove through high mountains and gazed at white clouds floating below, floating, as they were, untethered from everyday life. An Indian village sat on the mountainside, opposite the clouds. Peace, quiet, beauty, serenity. They breathed it in.

They came upon an Indian boy examining his damaged bicycle, his dark hair gleaming in the sun, his attention fully on the bike. Stopping to see if they could help, they found another language challenge, but with a few words and gestures among the three of them, they managed to communicate. The travelers learned that the boy lived in the village below and was trying to get there to have his bike repaired. They suggested tying it to the back of the car but couldn't find anything to tie it with. He gestured for them to go on. They thought they understood him to be telling them he'd be able to get to there by some other means. Maybe other people would come along, people who knew him and could help. Earline and Susan did finally drive on, although they didn't like leaving him there with his broken bike.

Their route took them past a mango grove where they stopped, taking the opportunity to rest under the inviting canopy of a huge mango tree. Sitting under the lush branches, they inhaled the soft air, thinking about and appreciating the varied landscapes they'd seen, this idyllic place in particular. Unable to resist, Susan tugged at a mango, eventually pulling the fruit from its branch. She peeled it, pulled off a piece for her mother and one for herself. Popping the morsels in their mouths at about the same time, they found themselves staring at each other's pucker. Bitter. Green. Far from ripe. No wonder it didn't want to come off its branch. But those two knew they'd have tasted it no matter what.

Back on the road, they drove within sight of Guadelajara but didn't go there, a decision Earline will forever regret. Then they continued west.

In Matzatlan they checked into a big hotel, right on the beach. The setting was gorgeous. Just what they'd expected. But the hotel itself fell short. The room's swamp cooler, which produced additional moisture, did nothing to mitigate the effects of the hot, humid air. The unhappy travelers dripped perspiration. A final insult came when someone lifted all of Earline's brushes, combs, and other toiletries. She suspected the maid, and they decided to find other lodging.

What was also galling was the money situation. Based on tales of how little the cost of living was south of the border, Earline had brought two hundred dollars, thinking that would be plenty for the two of them. It was turning out otherwise, with Earline suspecting fairly regularly that she'd been short-changed.

After leaving the big hotel, strolling down the beach, they came upon the Sands Motel. It looked inviting, so they went inside to find a pleasant surprise—the owner hailed from Boulder, Colorado. Earline felt at home talking with him and decided she and her daughter would be able to relax better there. The owner cashed her check, giving them more money to work with, and she and Susan moved their things in to stay for a while.

The timing of this trip, holidays for Mexican students, turned out fortuitously for Susan. Thirteen years old, beautiful and vivacious, she was surrounded by handsome, admiring young men for the rest of their stay. Earline had almost as much fun watching the dark-haired, dark-eyed young men entertaining Susan as Susan had being the center of so much delightful attention.

Driving back to Denver, they stopped in Tucson to visit Genevieve, an old friend from Empire days. Genevieve, a painter, lived in a lovely desert home with her husband, a retired doctor who also had taken up painting. Earline was particularly intrigued by Genevieve's adopted roadrunner, who would come by every day to be fed.

They saw more roadrunners and all kinds of desert animals on their visit to the Desert Museum outside Tucson and then were on

Chapter Twelve: A Mexican Interlude 137

their way back to Denver. Back to the apartment, back to making ends meet. But they'd had a lovely trip—new sights, relaxed days and nights, and a memorable time for just the two of them.

Chapter Thirteen

1966

THE DECADE OF THE '60S WAS A RUMBLE-TUMBLE TIME IN America and the world. Radical, ground-breaking ideas and social unrest, the likes of which Earline had not encountered before, formed the backdrop for her and her children's lives through those years. But 1966 stood out from the others for her out in several unforgettable, difficult ways.

The Second Indochina War, known to Americans as the Vietnam War, had become more prominent and more of an issue in the U.S. and was frequently in the newspapers and on television. Before its end in April of 1975, it would become an even greater issue. The seeds for U.S. involvement had been planted in the mid-1940s, but like most Americans, Earline thought of it as beginning only the year before with the deployment there of the first U.S. combat troops. Those fifteen thousand Marine troops joined the twenty-three thousand American military advisors who'd been there for years. And twenty-two-year-old Jesse Walker, family friend from Empire, was one of those first fifteen thousand. Earline worried from the start that Bruce would be sent to that distant southeast-Asian country, though Bruce, on the other hand, wanted to go. He enlisted for another year so that he could, and in spring 1966, as part of the 3rd Battalion, 5th Marines, that's where he went.

Remembering what she'd faced with family and friends during

World War II, Earline feared for her son's safety. Those earlier, indelible events and impressions now made Bruce's tour in Vietnam doubly worrying, worry that was only deepened by what she read in the paper and saw on TV.

In the midst of that worry, though, there came a bright spot at home—Carol's marriage to Ron Layton. Earline adored the bright, fun, attentive Ron and she was delighted that Carol, after several years of on-again, off-again antics with him, finally saw him for the exceptional young man he was. The young couple planned a small summer wedding to take place before Ron was to report for officer's training at Marine Corps Base Quantico in Virginia. He'd joined the Marine Corps several years earlier to help pay his way through the Colorado School of Mines, from which he graduated in May of 1966 with a mining engineering degree. Now he had a four-year commitment to the Corps to honor, and he held high hopes of flying jets for them.

Earline designed and made a graceful, elegant dress for Carol and helped her daughter plan the wedding. Bob flew in from Florida, Susan attended as bridesmaid, but due to his pressing military engagement on the other side of the world, Bruce couldn't be present. In a small church in Edgewater, Colorado, in candlelight and amid summer's daisies on the evening of July 16, 1966, Earline saw her daughter wed.

Immediately after the wedding, Carol and Ron drove to Virginia, stopping in Kansas City to see Ron's family, then on to Quantico. After dropping him there, Carol headed to Florida to see her dad and set up housekeeping near Pensacola Naval Air Station, where Ron would be stationed for his initial flight training.

Near Pensacola, the couple were only two hours down Highway 90 from Bob, and in the same town as Earline's youngest sister, Rubye. That fall, Earline was glad to know, for all of them, that Bob would drive over to spend Thanksgiving with Carol and Ron. But late on the day after Thanksgiving, Earline received a phone call from

Chapter Thirteen: 1966

Rubye. On his way back to Sneads, Bob had blacked out, and his truck had gone off Highway 90 and rolled. An ambulance took him to the hospital in the small, nearby town of Crestview. Earline later learned that Bob had had an electrocardiogram (EKG) there, but no one was trained read it. Because Ron had used the car to drive to the airbase and was out on an aircraft carrier all day, Carol had to take a bus to Crestview. Once there, she had to board another Greyhound, this time to carry the large envelope containing her father's EKG file to DeFuniak Springs. There were people there who knew how to read it. The information, however, would prove of no use. At midnight on November 26th, 1966, due to complications from undetected pneumonia, Bob's heart stopped beating. He was sixty-one years old.

Earline and Susan left for Florida right away. Bob was no longer her husband, but he'd been a significant part of her life, and she his, for more than twenty-five years. She felt the loss deeply.

After Bob's funeral, Earline and Susan returned to Colorado, Earline back to work, and Susan to finish her last year of high school. Bruce, who had returned to the U.S. for the funeral, ended up back at Camp Pendleton, to serve out his remaining few months in the Marine Corps. Some months earlier, he'd put in and been accepted for sniper school. That posting would have taken him back to Vietnam, but Earline had argued that Bruce was needed at home. And home was where they sent him.

Later, Earline read a letter from Bruce's commanding officer in Vietnam that he'd sent to Bob. First Lieutenant Kitrschki wrote

Dear Sir:

Just a few words to let you know of your son, Robert's progress. Since he joined the 81st platoon, he extended a year to go to Viet-Nam with us. His knee gave him sufficient trouble that he should have been discharged before we left CONUS [Continental U.S.], but he argued with the doctor and he was allowed to go with us.

He contracted pneumonia just prior to our departure for Viet-Nam and, although hospitalized right up until the end, he once again talked his way into going to war with our unit.

On every operation his knee has obviously given him trouble, but he never complains and never quits. He is my radio operator, so I know when he is "hurting." On Operation Colorado we were to go up to an OP [operation post] which had just been mortared. Your son was very sick at his stomach from bad water he had taken and was vomiting profusely but refused to leave me until I ordered him back down the hill to turn himself in to the Corpsman. He was back shortly, although I came off the hill myself, saying he was O.K. Between you and I, I seriously doubt he turned himself in in the first place.

As our 81 plt. communications chief he has done an outstanding job. As a Marine in combat he has proven himself time and again to be very courageous. Today we presented him with his promotion warrant to Sgt (Sergeant). We are proud to have him in the Corps and, especially, in our platoon.

—Respectfully,
Jame. J. Kirschki
1st Lt, 81 plt. cmdr

She was proud of what her son had done, but she thought it was enough. She wanted him home. With Susan in high school for another semester and Bruce back in the fold and finding his footing, Earline did the only thing she knew to do—she went on doing what could be done at work and for her kids.

Chapter Fourteen

The Hard Fact

Earline loved sales, and she was good at it. Even in retail sales in big department stores like J. C. Penney or May D & F, where she'd sold Singer Sewing Machines, she was good at and enjoyed selling things to people. What she loved best, though, was traveling and selling, that combination of seeing new sights and meeting new people in far-flung places. She liked the fun and the challenge in finding common ground with customers in order to know how best to talk about the product—describing its benefits just so, drawing them in, then closing the sale. Once out of it, she didn't miss the ever-present part of department store work—standing on hard floors all day, waiting for customers in a store with little to no natural light. The hard floors had already begun taking their toll on her back, and she was never one to flourish without abundant natural light.

Once Susan graduated from high school and prepared to leave for college in 1967, Earline found, for the first time in twenty-five years, she would have only herself to look after. She still needed to support Susan financially, but she wouldn't have to worry about where her youngest daughter was, whom she was with, or what she was doing. Susan would be sixteen hundred miles away attending Pensacola Junior College in Florida. She'd have no way of knowing what her youngest daughter was up to moment to moment, day to day. In some ways, it was a relief. In others, it was an even greater worry, but she realized it was one she could do nothing about.

Still, she had to work and the job she found just after Susan graduated from high school but before she left for college was in sales with a large photography outfit. That company, Fact, with headquarters in St. Louis and business all over the country, made photos for church directories and individual families. A huge concern, they operated through large department stores such as Sears, Wards, and occasionally independent stores in towns without the Sears or Wards—and in churches everywhere. With salespeople dispatched to travel throughout various parts of the country, the company could cover large swathes of territory.

Earline's territory, along with other Fact sales people, covered Texas, New Mexico, and other southwestern states, then later the northeast. She also always carried a stock of key chains that she got from a merchandiser in Denver. She'd found she could sell to stores such as Stuckey's, Horne's, and Skaggs, places that had funds set aside to buy "from the drawer." These sales provided Earline immediate cash for travel needs, carrying her through until she got her infrequent and meager Fact paychecks.

Earline was in Dallas when Susan came through on her way to Pensacola to register for and begin the fall college semester. Somehow her daughter found her way through the maze of freeways, overpasses, and heavy traffic to the motel where Earline was staying. Their reunion, although brief, was a warm and welcome respite for solitary Earline. For although she loved to travel, she missed being near family and friends.

Susan could stay only for the night, and she needed gas money to make it the rest of the way. Earline, scraping by as she was, didn't have it, but she knew she could get it. With characteristic resolve, Earline set out early the next morning for a nearby Skaggs and returned less than an hour later with fifty-nine dollars, enough to get Susan to Florida. With that stock of key chains to sell and her resourcefulness

Chapter Fourteen: The Hard Fact

and strong determination to make things work, Earline was able to stay on the survival side of the thin line between just making it and not.

Since she was in Texas that year, for Thanksgiving, Earline drove to Beeville where Ron and Carol were then living. Ron was completing advanced jet training there at the Naval Air Station, Chase Field. Her daughter and son-in-law rented an eccentric little wood frame house next to the railroad tracks whose walls shivered every time a train roared by. Several times a day.

Ron had invited several bachelor officers to join them for a holiday dinner of turkey and trimmings, and Earline captivated those young men, just as they charmed her with their polite manners and warm responses. Intrigued by her spirit of adventure, they quizzed her about the places she traveled, the people she met, how she managed on her own. Meeting a traveling saleslady in the 1960s was unusual in itself, and this one brought a combination of spunk and friendliness they found irresistible.

People and conversation spilled out of the little house, into the yard, under the big cottonwood tree Ron had to climb fairly often to retrieve their young cat, Kimmy. The warm, hazy day provided a perfect backdrop for this new community of friends to share a meal and a little portion of their lives with each other.

Earline could stay only a few days and then she was on her way again. A couple of weeks later she found herself in Carlsbad, New Mexico, a locale that struck her as singularly beautiful. The smaller, quiet town in country of such scenic beauty seemed to her the kind of place a person would want to live, maybe even more so in retirement. Decades later, she'll recall, " I remember eating in a restaurant. They had a whole side of that restaurant caged in with screen wire, and they had all kinds of birds there. I always liked to sit by the window to eat so I could watch the birds. Didn't matter what I ate, just so I could watch the birds."

She was in there Carlsbad when she got a call from the boss

to head to St. Louis right away. With her work finished, she left immediately, driving the more than one thousand miles in two days. Traveling across sagebrush hills and into wintry prairies, she arrived in St. Louis and at the hotel late the second night. Because she was out on the road for weeks at a time, she had everything she needed in her little Volkswagen Bug, including her supply of key chains, and she wanted to ensure its safety. She chose a spot under a light and asked the attendant if he'd watch over her car.

Two long, exhausting days on the road, and now it was after eleven p.m. To get to St. Louis as soon as possible, Earline hadn't stopped for dinner that evening and so, hungry and tired, she left everything in the car except the bare essentials—pajamas and toothbrush. At the registration desk she learned that the restaurant was closed but that she did have the option of ordering from room service. To that Depression-raised and hard-working woman, room service always seemed a luxury, one she didn't often splurge on, but this time she did. She chose a club sandwich from the small menu, hoping it would arrive quickly. Now in her room, while she had to wait for her sandwich, she didn't have to wait to get out of her travel clothes.

The knock on the door came just as she had shed slacks and shirt and pulled on her pajamas. Because in her rush to leave the car, she'd neglected to bring in a robe, she opened the door only slightly. She made sure there was just enough space to take the sandwich, hand the bellboy money, and preserve her privacy.

Bringing her handful of change back through the nominal opening, a quarter dropped and rolled a short distance across the carpet—just out of easy reach. Earline peered out into the hall, making sure the bellboy was gone, and opened the door slightly wider. She reached out to get the quarter, but it was just beyond her stretching fingertips Eyes on that quarter, she took a small step outside the door, and at that moment she heard it click shut behind her.

Stranded in the hallway in her pink, lacy shorty pajamas, no phone, nothing to hand but her sandwich, pragmatic Earline sat

Chapter Fourteen: The Hard Fact

down on the floor, propped her back against the wall, pulled her pajama top as far over her knees as it would go, and ate her sandwich.

After what seemed a long time, a figure stepped from the elevator and staggered toward her. A man, a drunk man. He stood chuckling at the scene before him. To Earline, determined to get into her room, the man was a potential asset. Ignoring his drunken snickering and using the most reasonable voice she could muster, she asked, "Will you go to the desk and ask the bellboy to bring a key?"

He responded by laughing outright. But, sniggering and snorting, he turned and wobbled down the hall and into the elevator. Earline could only hope he was heading to the lobby.

A few minutes later he was back. He stood a few feet in front of her swaying, stretched out his arm, and dangled his prize. She looked up to see light glancing off a key, her room key. The desk clerk had given her key to this drunk stranger. His laughter grated on her, but she could do nothing. She said nothing. Then, he turned, re-entered the elevator, taking her key, leaving her alone again in the long hallway.

There she sat, a desolate soul in shorty pajamas, in the late hours, desperate to be on the other side of the door, in her room, in bed, asleep. Long minutes passed, and the man reappeared only to laugh and leave again. With every minute seeming like an hour, Earline began resigning herself to a night in that hall.

But the man came back, and again, he dangled the key in front of her. Then he turned, walked to the elevator, stopped and looked straight back at her. Memories bubbled of the man looking in the windows of her house in Sneads and how she'd dispatched him. But here and now, she could do nothing. Finally, the SOB walked back to her, stood in front of her for a moment, and handed her the key. He was still giggling as he staggered away.

Once inside her room, she crawled into bed and tried to calm down enough to sleep. She eventually did sleep, which was good, because the next morning brought more misadventure.

Up early, Earline dressed and went down to breakfast. A hot breakfast, and the fact that she could eat sitting at a table fully dressed, not propped in the hallway in pajamas, was heaven to her. But that heavenly joy was not to last. Approaching her car, she gasped when she saw the broken wing window on the now forlorn-looking little Volkswagen. In disbelief, she pulled open the door to see what was there—and what was not. There was nothing. The Bug was empty. She looked in the trunk, and that was cleaned out, too. Her winter clothes and coat, the company's merchandise, everything gone. Adrenalin-fueled and with trembling hands, she pulled up the back seat and saw with relief that her three hundred dollars worth of key chains were there. At least the burglars had missed those.

She felt less than encouraged by the police's response. "This happens all the time," they told her. "You can't leave anything in your car. We'll try to find out who did it, but we can't promise anything."

Earline was miserable, and she felt violated. Her personal things stolen, the company's stock taken, and there she was in a cold, unfamiliar and hostile-feeling city. But she knew life and work had to go on and that an assignment awaited her in St. Louis before she struck out for the east coast.

Teamed with Jim, another Fact sales person, she was to work at a Catholic church in St. Charles, just outside St. Louis. A snowstorm raged that afternoon and evening, pretty much ensuring a white Christmas only a day away. It also meant a quiet evening for the two photography salespeople, who dutifully awaited the customers, who couldn't or wouldn't make it to them through the snowstorm.

They sat in the church's hushed space, waiting. They sat another long hour, until a hint of mischief grew in Jim's eyes. "I know where the priest keeps the wine."

He walked over to the organ, opened it up, and plucked out a bottle of wine. He and Earline still sat waiting, but happier, for the customers who never came.

The next day Earline left on another long drive, eleven

Chapter Fourteen: The Hard Fact

hundred-plus miles to Boston, her broken wing window temporarily patched with tape, and with the few clothes she'd bought to replace her stolen ones. She'll long remember the long, lonely stretches of highway she traveled, snow piled high on both sides, grey skies all around and a general sense of desolation permeating the air, inside and out of her little car. Years later she'll recall the New York throughway and finding nothing to eat. Every place she passed was closed up tight on that cold, dreary Christmas Eve, until she saw a truck stop on an overpass. One lone person manned the restaurant. "We've cleaned out today so we don't have anything except a cold hamburger."

Ravenous, grateful Earline told the man, "I'll take it."

Earline continued on, after dark reaching Batavia, which lay between Buffalo and Rochester. There she saw a single motel open, snow up to its eaves. She got a room and then asked about the other basic need—food. The registrar told her of a pizza place and gave directions. When she asked if he'd like to share a pizza, he didn't hesitate for a second.

She brought back the pizza, and the two sat by the fireplace savoring their Christmas meal and watching the roaring fire. After that long drive from St. Louis, the cheer and heat from the flames felt wonderful. Earline's well-practiced penchant for pushing away unpleasant and difficult thoughts made it possible for her to appreciate the warmth, the companionship, and the pizza.

She drove into Boston the next day on plowed but icy roads. Finding the hotel was first on her list, but food was again on her mind. She hadn't anticipated this continual difficulty in the holiday season, and her desire for a good meal was growing by the hour. After three or four attempts to reach the hotel, which she could see from the road but, thanks to the multiple exits and roundabouts, was hard to figure out, she discovered the way in. But, alas, her hoped-for meal was not to be. The only things on offer were a cold roll and an apple. Tired, hungry, far from home, Earline took what she could get and promised herself something better the next day.

The next morning Earline called Marian, another woman with the company who had already rented an apartment in Woburn. Also that day, another company salesperson, Rita, arrived in the city to join them. Marian's apartment was too small for three people, but she helped Earline and Rita find one for the two of them in the same building.

Of the churches she worked in, the Episcopal Church, the first built in Boston, was enormous and had a beautiful bell. Another, Methodist or Presbyterian, was Scottish and in Cambridge. She would remember the women who came in for their photos, who all seemed to have red, raw knuckles. She did well in the Cambridge church, liking it best of any she was in, and she especially liked the people.

Earline always appreciated interacting with her customers and listened with sympathy when, in the course of conversation, they told her of their worries and troubles. Once a woman came in and asked for every scrap of every picture of her husband. Earline thought she must have been around fifty years old, with gray hair and a nice figure. She told Earline that her husband had died recently, and those photos were the only ones he'd ever had made. He hadn't allowed anyone to take pictures of him before, but his wife had insisted that one time. Earline gathered up everything she had and also called the office to see if there were photos there. She gave them the woman's address and asked that if they found anything to send it to her. That day in Boston, she made another friend, one of so many across the country.

≫•≪

Years later it will still puzzle Earline how she managed to find her way around Boston. Despite its narrow streets, not squared off as in most cities, and tall buildings, she somehow managed to find all the churches.

Her time on the East Coast wasn't limited to Boston. She also

Chapter Fourteen: The Hard Fact

worked in surrounding towns, usually stopping at the Howard Johnson's near her apartment for fried clams on her way home at night. She thought they were the best fried clams she'd ever eaten. Some Sundays, when there was time and the weather permitted, she took in a few sights. One she remembered was the Old Sea Captain's statue, where the pilgrims first landed.

Earline had been in the Boston area for a little more than a month and had worked steadily during those weeks. Now, February 7th, 1968, she'd set up for her first night in huge, old Emmanuel Episcopal Church. Arranging an area for the photo packets, she took care creating a place to show photos to the customers so they could choose the ones they wanted for themselves and also make their selections for the church directory.

It was a quiet winter night, with the massive stone walls of the church seeming to deepen the February cold. To Earline, it felt as if all life were frozen. She heard the footsteps echoing along the walls and looked to see who might be her next customer. She watched as a man appeared, slowly and purposefully descending the stairs. Even from a distance Earline could tell something was terribly wrong with him. His ill-fitting clothes seemed better suited for warmer months. His feet splayed out to the sides as he maneuvered himself toward the distant corner where she sat—all alone. He glanced repeatedly at the clock, asking, "Is anybody else in this church?"

"Well," Earline improvised, "Father Frost is upstairs in his office. Go across this large area and upstairs to the auditorium."

The man didn't move. Earline elaborated her directions, not knowing if Father Frost was in the church, or if he even existed. "In the back of that auditorium you'll see a door, and that's his office."

Still the man didn't leave. He walked around, glancing at the clock, then at her. After what seemed hours, he finally turned towards the stairs, after, as Earline later described it, "He'd scared me till I had no sense."

Watching and listening, she waited for him to get up the stairs and into the auditorium doors. When she thought he was there, she grabbed her purse and the change box and bolted up the stairs, out the door, and to her Volkswagen. Her hands shook so badly she could barely get the key into the lock. But she did, and she was in the car and out of the parking lot like a shot.

The next morning Earline was on the phone to the home office. "I'm not going back to work in that church."

Coaxing came from the other end, resistance from Earline. More coaxing. And more. Earline relented. "Okay. But the only way I'll stay is if you get two men—not one, but two—to stand there by the door and not let the wrong people down the stairs."

The response, "If you'll stay and finish this, we'll get somebody to stay with you."

"Not one person, now. Two! Someone at the basement and someone at the rest room door."

She did return to the church, and two men accompanied her. It was then she learned that the janitor had found a man sleeping in the church, a man not likely to be the Boston Strangler, but a vagrant seeking a place to spend the night.

Despite the fact that this unsettling experience turned out to be less threatening than it seemed at the time, it was the final straw for Earline. For her own emotional well-being, she hadn't allowed herself to dwell on the lonely aspect of being on the road, of constantly being in unfamiliar surroundings. Nor did she acknowledge the continual stress of confronting wintry weather and difficult driving conditions, of wondering if she would find decent meals on a consistent basis, nor the long periods of waiting for customers to show up. Such thoughts she would put out of her mind, at least until their cumulative effects caused something in her to snap.

Her need for work and the absence of other opportunities had led her to Fact. Plus, she did like to be on the move, to travel. But now, the accumulation of the dreary, wearying, stressful conditions finally got to her. As was often the case, her decision came from her gut, and it was swift and irreversible. She'd change course.

Rita decided to return to the west coast and was thrilled to ride with Earline as far as Denver. With Friday, February 9, 1968, the last day of work, they set out for the west. Arriving in St. Louis on February 12, they stopped long enough to pick up their paychecks. Three days later, the two weary travelers finally reached Denver.

Chapter Fifteen

Messengers

January of 1969 brought the last issue of *The Saturday Evening Post*, Elvis Presley's comeback session for his new recordings, and the Beatles' last public performance. Except for Elvis, these events didn't hold much sway with Earline, but Carol's return to Colorado certainly did.

Carol had enrolled in the University of Colorado's Denver Extension to complete a degree while Ron finished his tour of duty in Vietnam. He flew an A4 Skyhawk, which he'd named Jefferson Airplane. Earline was working at World of Sleep, and mother and daughter decided to share an apartment.

With Bruce in gunsmith school in Lakewood and living in the mountains nearby, they saw him fairly often. Susan was still off in Florida, doing well and immersed in Asian Studies. Earline worried about her younger daughter being far from home, and she worried too about Ron, in the thick of the action in Southeast Asia. The war had only escalated, and the daily reports on the news were terrifying, with U.S. troop levels peaking at 543,400 during that year.

That spring day had been a long one. Only a few more steps, then she could take off her shoes, put her feet up, relax with a cup of tea, maybe with a little honey in it. It had been a long one at World of Sleep, but a productive one. There was a reason she was top salesperson, and it was the same reason she was tired. She put everything she had into her work. Doing so not only paid the bills, it also satisfied some small need to be recognized for what she was good at. She remembered the first time she'd gotten recognized for her sales, when she worked in sewing machines at the J.C. Penney store seven or so years ago.

As Earline started up the second and last short flight of stairs, something out of the ordinary caught her eye. Trousered legs. Someone was standing at the door of the apartment she and Carol shared. Two people, two young men, stood there, two young men wearing the well-known dress blues of the Marine Corps—sky-blue trousers, midnight-blue jackets, white peaked caps in their hands.

Seeing her on the stairs where she'd paused, the slightly taller one asked, "Is this where Carol Layton lives?"

Her response was slow and filled with suspicion. "Yes."

"May we come in? We need to talk to Carol."

"She's not here." Earline felt some relief that her daughter was out with friends from down the hall on this early spring evening, having drinks, listening to jazz.

"Who are you? I think we need to talk with you."

"I'm Carol's mother."

"Can we talk with you?"

"No."

If you don't hear the words, can something have really happened? If you refuse to believe something, can it affect you? Deny. Denying. Denial. These thoughts did not form in Earline's head, but in some form they lodged in her body, a body that would do anything to protect her children. The same body that had shot that man back in '52, the same body that had cared for and protected her children all along, as much as it could.

The men stepped aside as Earline put the key in the lock, turned it and went into the apartment. She tried to slip in by herself, but the men stayed right behind her and politely managed to get in, too.

Chapter Fifteen: Messengers

The other one said, "We have to read something to you."

It was then Earline noticed the papers in his hand.

The inevitability of the situation swiped at her. "Something's happened to Ron."

"Yes. And we need to read these papers to you."

Propelled by some deep, primordial force, she snatched the papers from his hand and threw them on the floor.

"I don't want you to tell me anything!"

She picked the one-hunderd eighty-pound man up and put him outside the still open doorway. Panting, she turned to see the other man picking up the scattered papers. His voice even, he looked at her and said, "Mrs. Wilson, we have to tell you this."

Her hands flew up to cover her ears, "No, I don't want to hear it."

But in the end, she did hear, and it was the thing she'd most feared.

≫•≪

SHE PHONED THE PLACE WHERE SHE KNEW CAROL WAS AND had her paged. When her daughter came to the phone, Earline kept her voice as level as she could. "I think you'd better come home."

They comforted each other as best they could, knowing the love they shared for Ron. For Earline, watching her daughter suffer this loss doubled her own suffering.

Ron's family came from Puerto Rico, where his mother and stepfather, Helen and John Armstrong, and youngest sister, Barb, lived at the time, and from Kansas, where his eldest sister, Pat, her family, and his father lived. The service was held at Fort Logan cemetery in Denver on April 17th. There was first a service at the funeral home, followed by the procession to the cemetery, the folding and presenting of the flag that had draped his coffin, the lone bugler playing Taps. The jets that flew overhead provided the dramatic endnote to a life that had been so full of hope, so full of promise.

That he was awarded the Distinguished Flying Cross, among many other medals and honors, made Earline proud, but it didn't bring her solace. Devastated but drawing on her deepest instincts for survival, Earline tried to put her mind toward her work, toward comforting her daughter, and seeing her through that trial, toward moving forward. What choice did she have?

Chapter Sixteen

The Call of the Road

During the early 1970s, with Richard Nixon as President, change and unrest continued to be a big part of the social landscape. In the decade before, the Equal Pay Act of 1963 and the Civil Rights Act of 1964 attempted to address inequalities that were common and accepted practice. The equal-pay issue directly affected Earline, for despite the legislation, women were among those still getting lower pay. Even in sales. But, intelligent and astute, she figured that by applying her sales talents to wholesale, she would fare better than in retail. And, she told herself once again, she wouldn't have to stand on those hard floors all day every day.

Although job stereotypes were being challenged during these years, the number of traveling saleswomen were few. But the road was again calling to Earline, and she responded. Stocking up on key chains and working for herself, she traveled around Colorado, down into the edge of New Mexico, throughout Wyoming, and even a little bit into Nebraska selling those mementos.

She was doing pretty well for herself, and when the time came to restock her supply, she went back to Meier & Frank in Denver. Rosemary, the owner's assistant, greeted her and, with no preliminary chitchat, said, "Mr. Goldberg wants to know what you're doing with all these key chains."

Suppressing the quips this question begged for, Earline gave an equally pointed response. "I'm going behind his salesmen and selling them. I guess they think since key-chains are a small item and they don't sell a lot of them at one time, they're not worth paying much attention to."

Rosemary acknowledged this bit of sales wisdom with a nod, then said, "Well, Mr. Goldberg wants to see you." She waved toward Al Goldberg's door to let Earline know she should go in.

Earline went in, and after greetings, Mr. Goldberg got right to the point: he wanted her to work for him.

She was pleased with another acknowledgement of her sales ability. On the other hand, she knew that, unfortunately, the kind of a job Goldberg was offering didn't mean money right away. But in her mind it did mean a chance for fair pay down the road, and she figured she could travel Wyoming for Al Goldberg and sell her key chains, and possibly other items on the side. She signed on.

Recognizing Earline's success and her potential for other regions, it wasn't long before Goldberg asked her to add Arizona to her territory. But she balked. "No way! It's too hot down there."

He persisted. She resisted. "I just won't go down there, Mr. Goldberg. I don't have the money to go, and it's too hot."

Countering, he offered an advance, a draw against her pay, of one hundred dollars a week, which would make the sales traveling possible, although not easy. At the time it sounded good, but decades later her assessment would be, "Big-hearted guy! I had to eat and sleep on one hundred dollars a week, plus buy gas. I could do it because I could find a lot of ten-dollars-a-night motels. But I couldn't stay out a whole week at that time. So anyway, that's what I did. Wyoming was the first state I went to."

She was to be paid once a year. The one hundred dollars a week was a "draw," or advance on her annual earnings. It was a job, she could travel, but the finances would prove challenging.

When soon after, the other salesman quit to go into business for himself down near White Sands, New Mexico, Earline, now the

Chapter Sixteen: The Call of the Road

lone salesperson, took over all the territory. She traveled through Colorado, Arizona, New Mexico, Texas, Oklahoma, Kansas, Nevada, and lower California, in addition to Wyoming. Given the small advance, expenses, and the commission from Al's merchandise, the only way she could make it work was to sell other products on the side. And she did—inexpensive, manufactured turquoise and gemstone jewelry from Leo Atherton, another souvenir merchandiser. Leo lived in Williams, Arizona, where he had his souvenir manufacturing business, Old West.

Earline's sales style was to try to see the product through the customer's eyes—what could pique a customer's interest in the merchandise, what might be helpful to her or him, and what would cause someone to buy from her. Her intuitive approach of stepping into the customer's shoes brought good sales. She realized customers needed an effective way of displaying goods, so she offered a rack when they bought six dozen key chains. This was one way to sell bigger quantities, sometimes clearing several hundred dollars at a time, which in turn, made travel easier, more do-able.

She also checked out how sales in general were going for her customers. By doing this and also looking around at their merchandise she once discovered that another salesman was taking Leo's jewelry and re-carding it with his own cards and name. She reported this misconduct to Leo and also began replacing the false cards with Leo's. Dismayed by these goings-on, she nonetheless stayed alert, finding evidence of the wrong-doing all the way into California.

Even given the sales from Leo's merchandise, life on the road offered few, if any, luxuries, and she had to stay focused on getting to as many customers as possible. This meant steady travel. And although she was on her own, she knew that she couldn't waste time. Sleeping nights, traveling and selling during the days, she rarely took time off. On Sundays, unless she had a long distance to drive or people to see, she did have an occasional rest. But, even at that, the KOA camp owners bought quite a bit, and she often saw them on

Sundays, her day of rest.

Driving the car she loved the most of all the cars she'd owned, the smooth-riding 1970 Chevrolet Impala, Earline motored along blue highways, across deserts, plains, mountains, through cities and towns, stopping at every souvenir shop, camp ground, drug store and any other place that sold souvenirs. Her beloved Chevy had a surfeit of space, and she needed every inch of it to carry her samples and stock.

Wyoming came to be a favorite, and not only for the scenery. Some of the prairies stretched long and flat, but then the gloriously rugged mountains rose in the distance, and Earline knew cooler air and stunning views were near at hand. But the big draw was the people she met. The warm, wide-open, come-on-in-and-have-a-drink-my-friend greetings delighted her. She felt welcomed, included, part of something—a community of friends. An inviting oasis for a solitary traveler.

At the Westerner in Dubois, every time she went in to meet a group, almost everybody bought everyone else a drink. There the bartender always asked her to play B3 on the jukebox, Hank Williams. When that spot closed, they'd all pick up their glasses and head to the other bar. Since she'd never been much of a drinker, she sipped her drink slowly. It wasn't the drinks, but the camaraderie she relished.

One time, relaxing in the company of these friends, she realized the time had slipped by, and she needed to be on her way to see customers in Rawlins the next day. The Dubois friends pleaded with her to stay. Earline, touched by their friendship, was tempted, but she knew that the almost two-hundred-mile drive would take the better part of four hours, and she should be on her way. Exchanging goodbyes with her friends, she got into her car and headed out of town.

Minutes later she glanced in the rear-view mirror; red lights flashed close behind her. She slowed down, pulled over, and watched as the flashing lights pulled over, too. A tall, lean state trooper slowly emerged from his car and walked up to hers.

"Are you Earline Wilson?"

Chapter Sixteen: The Call of the Road

"Yes, I am," she answered, perplexed.

"Good. Your friends sent me after you. You can come back on your own, or I'll escort you back."

Astonished, Earline turned her car around and drove back to town, the state trooper shadowing her. She rejoined the party, pleased to know her company was so valued. That she had to re-rent her room and get up early the next morning to be at that appointment was a price she willingly paid.

Another time the whole bunch piled into cars to drive up the mountain where they could better view a double rainbow. And once they went to a ranch that belonged to one of the men in the group. It was a real working ranch, complete with log buildings, bunkhouse, cowboys, horses and cattle. Seeing that place in its magnificent and rugged setting was a memorable Wyoming experience.

Sheridan was another town she much enjoyed. Known as the home of Buffalo Bill, it was full of friendly people. She sold souvenirs to Bernie, the mayor, who had a campground over in Ranchester. As had happened with so many of her customers, especially in Wyoming, they became friends.

It was late in the day on one wintry visit to Sheridan. Outside, rain hit the ground in little needle-nosed pellets. The sleet mixed with snow, freezing and swathing the roads in treacherous black ice. Earline and Bernie were having a bite to eat in a truck stop when Earline saw a young Indian woman come in the room. She looked hungry, something Earline couldn't bear.

"Have you had anything to eat?" Earline asked.

"No," came the reply.

Turning to Bernie, she said, "Bernie, buy this woman something to eat. She's hungry."

Bernie gave Earline an exasperated look that said "you and your Indians," but did as Earline requested.

Earline asked the woman where she was going and learned that she was headed to the reservation at Billings, Montana. She said she'd been in Sheridan two or three days hoping she could catch the mail carrier, who'd give her a ride up there.

Earline took all this in—the tired, hungry woman looking for a ride, unsure of when she'd catch one, the waiting, the unpredictability of her situation. She looked at Bernie and said, "I'm taking this woman home."

"Noooo. You're not gonna do that. You don't know that road." He proceeded to tell her how dangerous it was in the snow and ice storms.

Unconvinced, Earline said, "I've driven everywhere, Bernie. I can drive that road."

"Yes, but you've never driven on a road like that one."

Earline kept at it, telling Bernie she was going to drive to Billings, and she was going do it right now. Knowing she meant it, his concern got the best of him. "Well, hell! If you're going to do that, I'll take her! Come on. Let me gas up my car."

Not only did he gas up his car, but he prepared it in full Wyoming fashion—bowl of ice, a bottle sitting on the dash, and cups. Car and supplies readied, Bernie took the driver's seat, Earline took shotgun, and the Indian woman, Annie Long Hair, slipped into the back seat.

At first all seemed fine. They drove relatively smoothly for an hour or so, Bernie and Earline chatting some, with Annie barely speaking despite attempts to draw her into their conversation. When the car began to slip and slide, attention turned to the road and the car. They began to bump and sway.

"I believe I've got a flat tire," Bernie said, pulling over.

He stopped the car and stepped out onto the slick road. He saw that, yes, he did have a flat, and it was likely the result of the needles of ice protruding from the frozen road. He changed the tire while Earline and Annie sat in the car, afraid to speak, knowing Bernie wasn't a bit happy about this latest turn. He got back in the car and, wordlessly, drove on.

Chapter Sixteen: The Call of the Road

Soon the car began swaying again. Another flat. Bernie knew they were close to one of the few stations on that road and drove the short distance to it. It was closed. Since the hour was late, there were no lights on anywhere, not in the station, nor in the tiny house near it.

Looking right at Earline, Bernie said, "Maybe he will fix the tire, but you and she are going in there and wake them up. I'm not doing that."

Earline and Annie walked up to the house, hesitant, afraid to awaken whoever was inside. They knocked on the door. They knocked again. And again. Finally, a man came to the door, his reception anything but cordial.

Earline spoke up. "Well, we have a couple of flat tires out here, and we can't go any farther. Could you fix them for us? Bernie pays well."

"Pay" was the magic word, and it worked. The man repaired the tires, and the trio was on its way again. They had another flat, but the spare covered it. As they drew close to the first houses on the reservation, Annie spoke up, "Wait. Just stop right here."

As soon as Bernie stopped, Annie jerked the car door open and ran off into the night. No thank you, no goodbye, no wishes for a safe trip home. She was gone. Earline always wondered if she was getting out of Bernie's way as soon as she could.

But despite Annie's sudden departure, she saw how dismal the place was—the houses were all squatty, like sharecropper houses in the south, and it was cold. "Lord, you would have frozen to death in just a few minutes," Earline recalled.

The return trip went more smoothly, but the hundred-and-thirty-plus-mile drive on those bad roads was a long one. Tired, hungry, sleepy, Bernie and Earline made it back to Sheridan around daylight. They headed for the restaurant where Bernie and his friend Paul always ate. When they went in, they saw Paul, who wanted to know where he'd been.

"Oh, Paul. You know how Earline is about her causes. We've been up there on the reservation to take that Indian woman home."

"What Indian? What Indian woman?" Paul demanded.

"Hell, I don't know. What was her name?" he asked Earline.

"Annie Long Hair."

"Oh, Bernie! No that one! You didn't take that one up there, across the state line. She escaped from jail! In there for cutting up a woman with a razor blade. Bernie, you're the mayor of this town. Just wait until that hits the paper!"

Just then it came to Earline that she needed to be on her way. She knew Bernie had bought all the souvenirs he was going to buy and with the weather the way it was, it seemed best to get to the other side of the Bighorn Mountains as soon as she could. Stopping at the motel to pack up her souvenirs, she was on her way. Tired and sleepy, nevertheless Earline drove over the Bighorn Mountains, getting out of Sheridan as fast as her car would carry her. The snow was deep on the Bighorns, and figuring out where the road was and where the edge was took some attention. But she made it to Rawlins just fine. And Annie Long Hair? She never heard, and she certainly never asked.

Chapter Seventeen

On the Road to Sell

Earline traveled far and wide. At some point, she kept a wallet-style card file, which in later years would help fashion a geography of her sales travels. On a few of the business cards, she wrote notes, "Send order blank and pic of pottery" to the Nic-Nac Shack in Bullhead City, Arizona; "Jerry and Connie–new owners" of a KOA campground in Yermo, California; "rough stones," for the Apache Canyon Mining Company in Baker, California; "Wed. 9 a.m.," at Lake Mohave Resort in Bullhead City, Arizona. There were cards from more KOA campgrounds in various states—Victorville, California; Kingman, Arizona; Checotah, Oklahoma; Las Cruces, New Mexico; and, of course, throughout Wyoming.

Other cards suggested good souvenir shopping, and therefore likely sales: Apache Trail Trading Post in Apache Junction, Arizona; The Sutlery inc of the Cowboy Hall of Fame in Oklahoma, City; and one of her favorites, Happy Trails Gift Shop. And yes, it was a Roy Rogers enterprise, complete with Trigger, stuffed and standing in all his magnificence, in Victorville, California. Bun Boy Restaurants of Baker, California not only gave Earline good merchandise orders; it also offered good food. From Laughlin, Nevada, a Gammon Enterprises, Inc. card; Cherokee Trading in Barstow; Ponderosa Ranch in Incline Village, Nevada. The woman covered ground. She even traveled once to the Corn Palace in Mitchell, South Dakota, in the southeastern part of the state.

Built in a Moorish Revival style, the Corn Palace is decorated in, well, corn. The building is covered in murals and designs made of native corn and grasses, which are renewed each year based on local artists' designs. Earline remembered that the place had many visitors when she was there during the early 1970s. Around the time she found her card file in 2009, she learned that more than a quarter million people were visiting the Corn Palace each year.

When Earline left the Corn Palace one day in 1972, she was driving back across the vast Rosebud Reservation, home of the Rosebud Sioux Tribe, when she encountered a ferocious dust storm. The wind howled, "blowing like the devil," as she later described it. The air thick with dust and wind screeching across the wide-open space created a scene that made her long for a quiet room and a calming cup of tea. Instead, she got a scare when her car began coughing and sputtering. The sputtering increased, then the car stopped, right in the road. Looking around through the dust-clogged air, she confirmed what she already knew, that open prairie spread out around her for as far as she could see. A passing kind soul who knew about cars was her only hope.

She watched as several cars and trucks occupied by Rosebud Sioux drove by. At long last, a truck with more Sioux approached, and this time stopped. Several women climbed off the truck, walked over to the bank by the road and sat down, calmly perching on the high rise while the wind and dust swirled around them, catching their colorful clothes and long hair in a dance. She thought their clothes would blow off them.

Two men from the truck looked at her car, checking this and that under the hood. One took something off the carburetor and wiped it thoroughly with a cloth he had in the truck. The men had reason to be familiar with the effects of dust on carburetors. Out there it was basic, critical knowledge. Thanks to their knowledge and kind help, the car started, its cough a thing of the past as the

Chapter Seventeen: On the Road to Sell

engine purred steadily.

Earline felt so grateful for the rescue that, although she had no cash to offer, she wrote a check and asked them to accept it. They resisted. This was an act of common courtesy, one of them said, and they didn't want to be paid for it. But in the end, Earline won. They took the check, along with her profuse thanks. Later, she saw they had cashed the check, and for this she was also thankful.

❖

She traveled all over the West while working for Al Goldberg, but she also went to the east coast, to New York, for the big merchandise/trade shows. Alone on one trip, she managed to get from the airport to the hotel by herself, checked in and prepared for the next day.

The New York City trade show was held at the imposing Coliseum on Columbus Avenue, the structure a staggering three hundred twenty-three thousand square feet in all, with four floors for exhibition. On the cavernous main level, vendors packed the enormous space with their displays of jewelry, tee shirts, caps, cups, key chains, and other imaginative forms of souvenirs. Merchandise seemed to spill out of every nook, every cranny.

Sounds crowded every space, too. Everywhere was the buzz of excited vendors, buyers, casual lookers, the hum of humanity meandering through aisles, pausing at displays, conferring, acquaintances calling out to one another. Clatter and chatter filled the air.

Petite Earline, dressed smartly in an azure blue pantsuit, a color she knew echoed in her eyes, sat at her booth. She also knew she needed to draw attention to the gemstones Al had sent her to show and, most importantly, to sell.

She'd heaped the stones on the display table so they lolled in happy profusion across the white cloth beneath them. Silky tiger's eye with wavy bands of color, the blues and greens of chrysocolla—often mistaken for turquoise, tawny palm wood with its dark speckles. Potential customers strolled by, their eyes caught by the mass of little rocks. A few stopped, then moved on.

As a few more potential buyers approached, Earline reached into the mound and pulled out a blue-gray stone. She examined it for a moment then nonchalantly popped it into her mouth. She chewed, and her eyes closed as she savored the delicious rock. She opened her eyes, chose another, this one with a rosy glow, and slowly, deliberately dropped it into her mouth. Again she savored the unique flavor.

By this time a crowd had gathered, blocking the aisle. Several people wanted to eat a gemstone. Some started to reach for them.

"No, no! You'll break your teeth," Earline laughed, amazed and delighted that there still were so many folks willing to be gullible, just as there were decades ago when she was with the carnival.

Finally, she allowed one person to take one she'd pointed out. She didn't tell him some were gemstone candies she'd slipped in, and only she knew which were which. She cautioned him, "Now don't let it break your teeth."

Gingerly he raised the stone, placed it in his mouth, and with deliberation bit down. A twinkle crept into his eyes as he chewed.

In the end, she took an enormous order for gemstones. A Kellogg representative wanted several tons of them for Corn Flakes' trinkets. It was an order to match the size of this exhibition hall.

Later, when she reported to Al about it, he jumped up from his chair and exploded. "There's no way I can get that many gemstones! And then they'll just want more, and I can't get them. Those New York guys will sue hell out of me!"

"Well, Al," she said. "You sent me there to sell gemstones, and I sold them." It seemed to her the rest of the deal was his problem.

EARLINE'S PROBLEM UPON HER RETURN TO DENVER WAS OF another sort. She'd been renting an apartment with her friend Dot, but Dot had decided to go back to Reno. Earline took the opportunity to move out of their shared apartment, one she'd never much liked. While she was in New York, Susan, now at Colorado

Chapter Seventeen: On the Road to Sell

University, had moved Earline's furniture and clothes up to her own apartment in Boulder to keep until her mother returned and had a chance to find another place to live.

It was when Earline went to check on the vacated apartment that she encountered the immovable landlord—in the apartment. She asked for her sizeable deposit back, but he said no. He refused to return it. Depleted from several misadventures on the return from New York—freezing weather, delayed flight, lost luggage—she had little patience for the stonewalling from this lunk.

"This was supposed to be a cleaning deposit. The place is ten times cleaner than when we moved in," she told the man.

"That's what you say."

"You know it's true! We cleaned the carpet, painted the walls, everything!"

"You're not getting the deposit back."

Earline's eyes dropped to the carton of eggs that had been left sitting on the counter for the week she'd been gone. They were within easy reach.

"Okay. Then use the money to clean this up."

The first throw resulted in a satisfying splat as it decorated the freshly painted white wall. The second affirmed the first. But the third struck the landlord's forehead, a yellow stream coursing down his nose, dripping off his chin.

"You . . . You . . ."

But Earline didn't hear the rest. She was out the door. She never got her deposit back but, still, she got some satisfaction.

As far as trade shows and general sales went, Las Vegas was a big deal. Al would rent a room, which Earline would set up with their products, then customers would come in and buy. But one time Earline arrived at the Fremont Hotel the evening before she was scheduled to be there. The hotel was full, with no room for her. She found another room for the night, then returned to the

Fremont the next morning.

The hotel had only one driveway into the parking garage, requiring a guest to leave a key in the car so it could be parked out of the way if necessary while she registered. Earline left her key, but said to the attendant, "Don't move my car. I'll be right back." Taking ten minutes or less to register, Earline returned to the driveway.

Not seeing it, she asked, "Where's my car?"

"I don't know, " the unfamiliar attendant answered. "We just changed shifts."

She persevered. "My car was right here. I was coming right back as soon as I registered."

Another person chimed in, "I saw a man come out of the hotel and get in your car and drive off."

Earline's temper kicked in. "Don't tell me any stories, just get my car. I have to get to the airport and pick up my boss!"

"No. I'm not telling you a story. He had on a blue suit. He just got in your car and drove off."

Then it registered. She'd been set up. She'd been there last evening when the earlier shift was on, and that shift was still there when she arrived again that morning. But now they were gone. And so was her car. Was it a friend of someone on the shift? Was it an attendant? But in a suit? And where was the car? Knowing she'd be staying in the Las Vegas area for a while, several months at least, she'd moved out of her apartment and had everything she owned in that car—all of her clothes, many of which were brand new and special, her movie camera, her Indian bead collection—and seven thousand dollars worth of Al Goldberg's souvenirs. Of the old clothes she'd kept, she was wearing her worst ones, comfortable clothes for driving. She had nothing else. Everything was gone and without a trace.

Beside herself with anxiety, Earline called the airport to let Al know to take a taxi to the hotel. Someone else called the police.

Al's anxiety matched Earline's, although his was more obvious; she never liked to show her feelings, her vulnerability. But Al was

Chapter Seventeen: On the Road to Sell

a different matter. Nervously scratching his legs, he fretted about the lost souvenirs, the lost opportunity, and his reaction made her want to scream. She knew she had to do something about her own bottled-up nerves, her tension and apprehension. Finally, she called a doctor who came and gave them some tranquilizers. This helped Earline, but still Al sat and scratched.

What a jam. A merchandise showing with no merchandise, and the warehouse a thousand miles away. This was a real muddle to be sorted out, and there she was with no decent clothes, no car, and spent nerves. Add in a frantic boss and a defensive hotel staff, and she could only feel grateful for the small mercy of tranquilizers.

Resolution came slowly. Rosemary shipped more merchandise right away, but the other issues took longer to resolve. The hotel reimbursed Earline minimally for her clothes, and they paid her hotel bill. Four decades later, she'll still think maybe she should've padded that bill. As for the car, working through the process with the insurance company, Earline managed to get another car in Las Vegas, a station wagon this time.

In the midst of their turmoil, their merchandise show went on. Their Indian jewelry, silver dollar belt buckles, bolo ties, and bracelets, and the special-order key-chains, tee shirts, and other souvenirs and trinkets with individual company logos, when they got them, brought the customers in.

Later on, at Al's request, Earline had rented a house in which she could live and also use one of the bedrooms as a showroom. She secured some blocks and boards for display shelves and arranged the room to show the merchandise to its best advantage.

She liked that house, with its beautiful, soft bluish-green, sea-foam and pinkish-lavender colors, which created a calming environment for her personally, and for her work. But, nice as it was, being in the house and having to replace the car and clothes couldn't bring Earline peace of mind. The experience of the theft had shattered her. It was a final straw in the accumulation of stresses, uncertainties, aloneness.

She had what she herself described as a nervous breakdown.

Her condition was doubly complicated by the physical setup with the merchandise. On the one hand, she had the wares on display in the house, convenient for her, but she still needed to go out and get customers, take samples to show them. People didn't automatically go to her. That wasn't how things were done in Las Vegas. For the most part, those who sold souvenirs at retail had to tend to their shops by day and lead their private lives at night, so they needed someone to come to them. But she simply could not go out and sell "to save my soul," she would recall. She couldn't make herself do it. Consequently, her sales fell. She found Las Vegas a "nerve-wracking town." She hated it, hated what had happened to her there, hated living there.

To try to make it as bearable as possible, Earline encouraged Susan and her wonderful boyfriend Ric Rawlins to come out for a visit. She also invited Carol to come. Visiting at different times, Susan and Carol brought with them some sense of connection and home, but what comfort they provided was only temporary.

Earline finally packed up and left that city of bright lights, seeking a less alien environment, a place where some family and friends were nearby. That road to sell had sold her out.

Chapter Eighteen

Work, Friends, Life

More than she would have liked, work continued to define Earline's life, in large part determining where she lived and how she spent much of her time. From a vantage point more than three decades on, she wouldn't quite remember the exact sequence of jobs after the sales travel ended around 1973; however, she would remember the essence of those years and, in some cases quite clearly, the various forms her dissatisfaction took with many of the jobs.

Given her economic situation at the time and the dearth of opportunities, she felt she often had to take what was available and offered; she was surprised and gratified that she was always offered a job by a business acquaintance. Apart from that bad Las Vegas experience, she could no longer deny that the back and leg problems she'd developed from lugging heavy sample and merchandise cases made sales traveling out of the question. But sales it continued to be for the ever-formidable saleswoman, only now she needed to sell mostly in one place.

From her early days a traveler at heart, Earline had found all the sales travel stimulating and, in her outgoing way, had developed countless friendly relationships with her customers. But with work and travel consuming most of her time, and certainly her energy, staying in touch with old friends in those years proved just too difficult—cell phones and email wouldn't be part of her life for another thirty years. And so, besides the effect on her back and legs, those itinerant years had taken their toll in yet another way.

Once settled back in Denver, she found some of her friends had moved away. And in other cases, as with much else in life, what is not nurtured will decline, and she found she had little in common with a number of acquaintances who were nearby. Of her friends, the ones she carried most dearly in her heart were those from Empire, from her all too brief time there back in the 1950s. Her memories of Nell, Virginia, Dr. Jo, Eula and others remained vivid, and she often replayed the fond images of their easy days of laughter and friendly banter. The sense of community she felt there among them had been unprecedented in her life—the birthday-lunch celebrations, casual coffees at the Hard Rock Café, the almost daily telephone or face-to-face conversations to check in or share a bit of news. And though she didn't know it then, that brand of camaraderie she so cherished was not to be repeated.

She did, though, occasionally see some of those old friends. Dr. Jo had moved to Denver, much to Earline's great joy; they would have lunch, go to a hockey game or attend a concert together. And while Earline loved those times, for her, making a special effort to get together differed from being in each others' lives on a daily basis. Virginia, Nell, Eula and others she saw when she could. Sadly, they would all pass away during the 1970s and 1980s.

She'd stayed in touch with little Peggy Chavez, who wasn't little anymore but had grown into a pretty teenager, and who would, a few years later, help Earline with a major project down in Florida. June, the friend from her brief Parks Business School experience, and pal Dot were still in her life. Earline would later lose touch with Dot, but June would remain an in-touch friend.

It was with Dot that Earline would have a few memorable adventures, often without looking for them. Like the time the two drove back from Reno through Wyoming. They'd stopped for the night

Chapter Eighteen: Work, Friends, Life

and were walking back to the motel after dinner when Dot set off the fire alarm and landed in jail. Earline had had to do all the pleading she could with the sheriff to get bail set for her friend.

But it was their trip to Baja, Mexico that gave real meaning to the term "adventure" for those two. Earline, with her cat George, drove from Denver to Dot's in Reno, Nevada. From there, the three continued on to San Francisco, where they left George in the capable hands of Susan and her roommates. Earline and Dot were headed south down the California coast, bound for a holiday in Baja.

Susan, that full-of-surprises younger daughter, by that time had completed a Master's degree at the California Institute of Asian Studies and a law degree at Hastings Law School in San Francisco, and was now working at the Occupational Health and Safety Administration as a regulations editor. While the position didn't thrill her, she'd stay there until she figured out her next move.

Meanwhile, Susan and her roommates were delighted to have George, the charismatic kitty, as a houseguest. He was a special one, that cat; he would come running to Earline or whoever called him, throw himself down at the person's feet and await petting. Commenting on George and other cats Earline had, Dot once wondered aloud, "Earline, how in the world do you get these cats? They do anything you tell them to!" Seeing George happily settled in, Earline and Dot headed out in high spirits, driving in Dot's new red Chevrolet Impala. Their intent was to go all the way to land's end, to Cabo San Lucas.

All went well until, about the time they were a third of the way down the Baja peninsula, with the Impala's gas gage hovering on empty, they began to worry. Every gas station they came to had the same problem—no electricity and no way for the pumps to pump to replenish the holding tanks. But the travelers kept going, unaware that the frequent power outages in those parts could go on a long time. As they neared the little village of Mulege, right on the Sea of Cortez, they realized their luck, and their tank, had completely run out.

Pulling in at the first place they saw, a bar and motel, they breathed a joint sigh of relief that they'd found a sanctuary and wouldn't be stuck out in the middle of the desert without food or shelter.

Making the best of an unexpected situation, something at which Earline and Dot had always seemed to excel, they settled in for an entertaining time. The motel had a small generator, so they had some conveniences. And, what they didn't know was that they'd landed in a place favored by Hollywood actors and other wealthy industry types. They learned from their favorite bartender that the high-flyers, coming there to get away from it all, would land at the small local airport, often in their own planes. One night, they were sure Elizabeth Taylor came into the bar and sat quietly in the corner. Other nights, sitting in the same bar, Dot and Earline spent time speculating on who was there. Given the scant lighting and a celebrity's wish for anonymity, who could tell just who might be sitting across the room from them?

But the novelty of the place and their situation did finally wear off, and after more than a week they began to worry. They needed to get back, Earline to her work, Dot to her own commitments. Someone told Dot to go to where the airplane gas was stored at the airport; there was a private generator there and, possibly, she could get some of that gas put in her car. That's where she went, and she did get the gas. With the Impala fueled on one-hundred-octane gas, they literally flew back toward the border. Then it was quickly on to Reno, where Earline picked up her car and drove to San Francisco to fetch George.

It was a long ziz-zag of a haul from San Francisco back to Denver. After a brief overnight stop back at Dot's in Reno, Earline and George drove on to Williams, Arizona, where she was to pick up some Indian jewelry from Leo Atherton. She'd now driven all night and was tired. Just in Death Valley, she made a stop for gas, where she stretched and rested before being on her way again.

Chapter Eighteen: Work, Friends, Life

It wasn't until she was a hundred miles down the road that she thought about checking on George. She figured he'd been sleeping in the back, but a thorough search turned up no George. She thought he must have crawled out at the gas station.

With no time to drive back the hundred miles to look for him, Earline called the resourceful Susan. In turn, Susan called the sheriff in the town where that station was located, who in turn got hold of a bunch of young boys, who then went out searching for the lost cat. And they found him.

More accurately, George had found a couple who said he'd walked up to them and thrown himself at their feet. They were smitten by the friendly white kitty with one yellow ear and asked if they could keep him, explaining that they'd been wanting a white cat as a companion for their black dog.

Having to admit to herself, reluctantly, that she just didn't have the time to drive back the hundred miles to get him, Earline agreed to let the couple keep him. At least he would have a good home, she reasoned, though she sorely missed that special kitty.

She drove on, lonely now, thinking of George and their times together. A memory of him in the role of watch-cat came to mind and made her smile. The incident happened when she and George were staying at family friend Ric Rawlins' cabin in Pinecliffe, Colorado. Ric was off working on movie sets, and he'd told Earline she could use his cabin anytime she wanted. In need of a quiet getaway, Earline had taken George and gone up to the cabin to stay a few days.

The place, a lovely old log cabin Ric had renovated with great care, sat in a remote spot on the creek near Pinecliffe and not far from Miz Scofield's Wee-Two Ranch, where Earline and her kids had spent part of their summers back in the mid-'50s. As part of the cabin's refurbishing, Ric had built a loft bed, a kind of platform, suspended by chains from the ceiling. There was a ladder to get up there, and above it, on the wall, hung a rifle.

One night as she slept, George leapt from the bed, darted down the ladder and took up racing round and round the room. About the same time, Earline heard a "BLAM" outside the window, as if someone had slammed a big piece of tin again the window or side of the cabin. Whoever or whatever it was had found the back door and was trying to open it. The door handle was wiggling back and forth.

With George running wild, Earline grabbed the rifle and stole down the ladder. She managed to make a call to the sheriff and, mercifully, the dispatcher picked up on the first ring.

"Just hold on, don't hang up," the dispatcher said. "Do not hang up! The deputies'll be there in just a minute." Then, in minutes, "Okay, they're there," the dispatcher told her. "You can hang up now. They know you're in the cabin and they're checking out the property."

Within a few minutes, the deputies were knocking on the door, and when Earline opened it, they pointed their flashlights toward themselves so she could see their uniforms.

"Well," one said, "there was a guy out there, but outside the fence and not on this property. We talked to him, but we couldn't arrest him without any evidence he was the one trying to intrude."

"If he's not on the property," the other deputy said, "the law says we can't arrest him."

A stupid law, she thought, but did not say; anyone can run past a fence. But she thanked the deputies for their help, and especially for their quick response, and saw them off.

The rest of the night passed without incident, though Earline did not sleep. Her body tensed for the intruder's return, she lay in bed, her mind alert to every sound. George the watch-cat, however, found nothing to keep him awake and curled up beside her to sleep through the rest of the night.

Two or three days later, she heard a knock on the back door. Through the window of the door, she saw a man and thought, Uh-oh. She stepped closer, but didn't open the door.

"What do you want?"

Chapter Eighteen: Work, Friends, Life

"Open the door," came the reply.

"No. What do you want?"

"Open the door. I want to talk to you."

"Talk to me through the door."

"I just came over to tell you," the man said, "that the next time somebody's trying to get into the cabin, instead of calling the police, call me. I live in the cabin straight up the mountain from here."

Earline thought about the Pinecliffe area. She knew there were cabins sprinkled up and down the mountainside, and she could well imagine this man with binoculars or a telescope looking down on everything going on below. Then, in the next breath, the doorknob was shaking; the man was trying to get in.

Earline, who was wishing she had more protection in that cabin than one white cat, called out, "Get away from here right now, or I'll call the sheriff!"

Finally, he did leave. And so did Earline and George. She packed up, never to return, despite Ric's insistence that she should think of the cabin as her own. Long after that, she could still conjure up an image of that man sitting up the hill, binoculars in hand, waiting for her to come back.

❧•❦

Whether her jobs saw her selling on the road or standing in stores, one thing remained constant: Earline's spunkiness. Often times this personality trait served her well, sometimes not so much.

She would always remember Vern, her boss at Singer telling her, "Earline, I knew when I hired you that you were high-strung and temperamental. That's why I hired you. You wouldn't be worth a damn to me otherwise."

Taking a job with Bernie Niles and his Ready-Spuds in Denver, she sold potatoes, hams, and other foods. This job had its stresses, including physical security. The time she told Bernie she wouldn't go into a particular neighborhood because it was dangerous, he tried to give her some safety lessons.

"I'll show you what you can do in case anybody ever comes up behind you and tries to touch you. When they put their hand on your shoulder," he said, "you just do like this," and he demonstrated a subtle shoulder movement.

"I don't believe that'll do it, but let me try it on you," Earline proposed.

"Okay, but don't shrug your shoulder hard. Just a tiny bit."

Afterward Earline would say she thought she was shrugging just a tiny bit, but the effect of throwing her boss half-way across the huge warehouse room and onto the concrete floor made her wonder.

She hurried over to where he lay, offering to help him up. "Oh god, Bernie, what did I do to you?"

Bernie got up without saying a word. "After that, he wasn't too happy; he wouldn't let me practice on him anymore. He did tell me how to do karate chops by using the side of my hand—make my hand stiff and whack 'em right under the ear, about the middle of their neck," she remembered. "And he told me to stick my fingers in their eyes. But, no more practicing."

That spunkiness, forged from her ready empathy with customers, her quick temper, her desire to be self-sufficient and to take care of herself, made for an attention-grabbing blend of characteristics in her various jobs. And when the economy was bad and jobs scarce, this blend could come into play in dramatic ways.

For a time she sold furniture for C. D. Brooks, a sharp businessman who would become a friend. Her supervisor at that store was Ed Snow. Another of the several salespeople there was a guy named Sam. Unlike Earline, who liked to let people look around a bit first, Sam's approach was to claim a customer as soon as possible. But one day, Sam claimed too much.

A young couple came in to look at refrigerators. Before they had a chance to look much at all, Sam ran over and began his pitch. About the same time, a woman came into the carpet department, which

Chapter Eighteen: Work, Friends, Life

wasn't all that far from appliances. She gazed around for a moment and then caught Earline's eye. But before Earline could walk over to her, Sam, having made a brief initial contact with the refrigerator couple, scurried over to intercept the carpet woman. Shooting Earline a too-familiar look that said, "This one's mine," he pushed her aside.

Fed up with his antics, Earline's spunkiness turned to anger, and it took over. She felt her hand go rigid, rise up, then come down on Sam's neck. His eyes opened wide, his own hand came to clutch his neck, and he moved toward Ed. She turned toward Ed, too, but stopped and turned back. That first strike had felt so good, she decided she'd do it again, this time on the other side. She did. He stared at her for a moment, then ran off to Ed, wailing, "She hit me! She hit me! She didn't just slap me. She balled up her fist and hit me!"

The other three salespeople had stopped what they were doing to stare, but only momentarily. Soon they were clasping their sides, all three doubled over with laughter. Sam had finally gotten his cut of the action.

When Ed Snow talked with her about the incident, he used his nickname for her, saying, "Stinker you really got him! You just wound up and walloped him."

The next day was Earline's day off. When she returned to work, C.D. Brooks asked her to come to his office. "Want to tell me what happened?" the store owner asked her.

"No, not really."

C.D. waited.

"Okay, I hit him," she said and awaited her punishment.

"Well, you won't have to worry about him anymore. I fired him."

Gape-mouthed, Earline looked at him.

"It's better it happened this way," C.D. said. "If Ed or Chuck had had to do it, it would've been much worse."

AS DID SO MANY OF HER JOBS, FURNITURE SALES WORK required

standing long hours on cement floors. The toll those standing hours took on her back resulted in multiple back problems, which ultimately required serious surgery.

Given the limited employment options in Denver, Earline had decided to try her luck back in Florida and, despite the serious nature of that back surgery, soon after she made her way back to Sneads, in 1974. She returned to live in the cottage Bob had built behind the store building he'd used off and on during the late 1950s, until the end in 1966.

Ric Rawlins, of Pinecliffe cabin fame and a close friend of Susan's and the whole family, was a talented carpenter and came all the way down to Sneads to help transform the building into a restaurant. Earline did her share, too. She would later recall, "I sat on that cold, icy concrete floor, in February, after having that surgery and put that plastic flooring down, and then I opened the restaurant."

For a solid year, she worked her heart out — cooking breakfast and lunch, and sometimes dinner for certain customers, ordering food, keeping track of the business accounts and books, and serving, too. For a few months, Peggy Chavez came down from Colorado to help her out. But, once again, Earline was standing on a concrete floor for hours, and again it was taking its toll on her body.

"I enjoyed that restaurant," she would say of that time, decades later, "but it worked me to death. Had all those people from everywhere coming in. But, I was going nowhere with it. I wasn't making enough to live on."

Finally, accepting the financial reality of it all, she closed the restaurant and moved back to Denver, returning to work for a company she'd worked for briefly a few years before. The job brought in enough money for the time being, and it also brought an opportunity for a little settling of scores.

Back in 1973, when she'd left Las Vegas, she'd had a major disagreement with Al Goldberg about the money Meier & Frank owed her. That disagreement had turned into a lawsuit, and Earline had

Chapter Eighteen: Work, Friends, Life

never been satisfied that justice had been done.

Now selling gift items and souvenirs again, this time for Kevin & Co., Earline capitalized on the contacts she'd made while working for Meier & Frank, especially those in Arizona and Wyoming. Word got around at the merchandise shows that she was back, so many of her old customers stopped by to see her. And she got their orders, which meant that Al didn't, which eventuality had the flavor of justice for her.

After the stint with Kevin & Co., it was back to working furniture sales for her friend C. D. Brooks. He'd wanted to sell his smaller store and open a larger one, so Earline kept the smaller store going during the transition.

She was to work with C.D. again later too, but in an entirely different business— selling plots at a large Denver cemetery. In characteristic Earline style, whatever she was selling, she went all out. And in the cemetery field it was no different. Three decades later, Carol's friend Roger Rountree, then a detective with a local police force, would remember Earline asking him to "smoke a few guys" so she could increase her sales.

≫•≪

EARLINE WAS A BIG HIT SELLING FURNITURE AT THE GRAND Denver Dry Goods in Aurora. The store had recently opened, and it turned out she was selling furnishings they didn't even have in stock yet. One day the store supervisor called her into his office.

"I want to know why you're selling furniture and nobody else is."

She explained what seemed obvious to her. "I charge them a deposit, so they know they've bought something. Somebody comes into the store and you show them everything you've got. They'd like to have this and they'd like to have that, but if they don't put money down on it, they go away and don't come back. Even if they're rich." She thought it funny to be schooling her boss, but she went on, "So I write up a ticket and have them sign it, and I get a deposit. I don't know why the others aren't doing this. All I'm doing is sealing the deal."

Earline had no idea she wasn't supposed to charge a deposit, that it was against store policy.

The supervisor looked at her. "Where'd you learn this?"

"I've worked in more places than you'd ever believe," she said, "and I know how to get that money."

"You know, this makes sense to me."

Shortly after that and thanks to Earline, all the Denver Dry stores now had a new policy.

Chapter Nineteen

Fishing Buddies

Earline spent the summer of 1980 looking after her future grandchildren. At the time, she couldn't know Rick and Shari would come to be part of her family, that Carol and their widowed father, Chuck, would marry in the next year. But she knew she loved those children. Towheaded Rick at six years old and Shari at nine captured Earline's heart, just as they delighted in her—and Frosty, her precocious, fluffy white cat.

That summer also came to be known and treasured in Earline's fishing annals, for that was when she and Rick became fishing buddies. Shari ventured out with them on a few occasions but, at the time, she preferred the company of other pre-adolescent girls. It would be a couple of decades before she gave much attention to fishing, and then only in passing.

Whether they headed for the mountains or Sloan's Lake on Denver's edge, Earline and Rick relished every fishing opportunity. Earline taught Rick the sport's ins and outs—how to bait a hook, which bait to use, which tackle to use in particular streams, ponds, and lakes. Little did she suspect that later on fishing would play a central role in Rick's personal and professional life, that he would be featured in fishing and outdoor magazines, that he would have his own weekly television show, with fishing a part of it.

In the mountains, they'd sometimes go near Miz Scofield's ranch, below Ric Rawlin's cabin. Although the water was swift there, it trickled between the many big boulders, forming pools, so Earline didn't have to worry about six-year-old Rick's getting swept away.

One clear, crisp day, they were fishing the lake at the top of Loveland Pass in the north-central Colorado Rockies. That was a spot she and another long-time fishing friend, Wilbur Colvin, favored. The sky was the kind of infinite blue seen only at those high-mountain altitudes—this one, eleven thousand nine hundred feet. A number of other anglers were there, but no one was catching anything. The intense sun moderated the effects of a nippy wind as Earline set Rick up with his equipment, then set up hers. Right away, soon as their lines went out, they both starting pulling in the fish. Earline thought of something else that might work even better and switched the two of them over to fly and bubble, a combination of a wet or dry fly and small plastic bubble used especially for catching lake trout. They both continued "to hammer them," as Rick will remind his fishing buddy thirty years later. The other puzzled anglers asked the two how it was they were doing so well. Earline just smiled, and Rick followed her example.

Another day found them outside Colorado Springs at a pay-to-fish pond with friend Paul Kyle. The well-stocked pond held beautiful golden trout and lots of native-Colorado rainbow trout. A delighted Rick caught a bunch of them, resulting in an equally delighted Earline.

With Sloan's Lake only a short drive from home, they often went there. Once Rick had a big one on the line, but it got away. Earline took a picture of Rick showing with his hands just how big that fish was. She will always keep that photo.

A year or two later, when Earline was back in Florida for a spell, Rick went to visit for a few weeks. Naturally, they headed to nearby Lake Seminole to try their fishing luck, stopping along the way to pick blackberries. The fishing was good, and as a bonus, Rick found a big land turtle, which he adopted for his stay.

The lake offered good swimming, too, and not just for boys. Once, out for a dip, Rick looked to his side and was startled to see an alligator swimming much too close by, its eyes bulging out of the water. When it dove under the water, Rick's adrenaline kicked in and he headed for safety. Earline, whom Rick called GrannyMa, laughed about how he walked on water getting back to shore.

GrannyMa and Rick enjoyed other bodies of water, too. Trips to Panama City Beach and to the clear springs, Blue Springs and Wakulla Springs, figured in their swimming fun. The high platforms with their diving boards positioned over the deepest part of the springs proved a thrill for Earline's GrannySon. She taught him to carry rocks when jumping from a high place into the water. As Rick would later remember, "Throwing the rocks down to break the water's surface was the key to not ending up with stinging feet."

During the visit, Rick learned other tricks from Earline, like how to make the call of the Bobwhite quail, whose "bob-bob-white" is ever-present in that area. And with so many back roads around, Earline taught Rick to drive; the boy was just tall enough to see over the steering wheel. Earline will long remember one outing when an oncoming car rounded the corner of the lane they were on without slowing, coming right at them. She was yelling, "Stop, Rick! Stop!" Somehow the cars got around each other, she'll later recall, "but it sure gave me a heart attack."

When Rick dubbed Earline "GrannyMa" on this trip, neither realized that name would stick. Almost three decades later, he'll speak of her to his little daughter, Mackenzie, as her Great-GrannyMa. Rick and his wife, Kim, pregnant with Mackenzie, would visit GrannyMa just three months before their little girl was born. Shari would stay in touch, too, regularly sending Earline photos of her children, Tatum and Riley. Theirs continues to be a lasting bond, long after Carol and Chuck themselves parted ways.

EARLINE LOVED HAVING CHILDREN IN HER LIFE, ESPECIALLY

now that hers were grown and busy. In the early 1980s, having completed undergraduate and graduate degrees in Eastern thought, Susan had finished her law degree, specializing in civil rights law. After that, Earline had figured nothing her younger daughter would do could astonish her. But she was wrong. Susan joined the U.S. Army, was commissioned a captain and promptly assigned to the Adjutant General's office in Colorado Springs.

Earline knew one of Susan's law professors had suggested she join up because practicing for the AG would get her significant courtroom experience, something difficult to come by as a beginning lawyer in private practice. Earline also understood that the move would give Susan the opportunity to stand up for those whose voices wouldn't be heard otherwise, a cause close to her daughter's heart and one of the primary reasons she'd specialized in civil rights law. In typical Susan fashion, she worked all hours at her job, leaving little time for much else, and she was wildly successful in that role. The Colorado Springs *Gazette Telegraph* did a major spread on Susan and her efforts, focusing some on her Native American heritage through Earline's mother. Earline was proud of, and a little awed by, this whirling dervish of a daughter.

When Susan asked Earline, who was living in Denver in those days, to move in with her in Colorado Springs, Earline happily accepted. That put Carol, and most importantly, Rick and Shari, only a scenic hour's drive up I-25, but Bruce and Suzanne were still in the Alaskan bush on their homestead.

It would be just a year or so before Earline would be up there in the Alaskan wilds, too, although she'd miss her fishing buddy, Rick.

Chapter Twenty

North to Alaska

July 15, 1981, brought Earline a new grandson. Bruce and Sue, married for nine years and on their homestead in Alaska, now had a healthy, beautiful boy. Earline thought Zachary Dane Wilson a most welcome addition to the family. Another in the younger generation, which by then already included Rick and Shari.

The next year, during the summer of 1982, Bruce and Sue asked Earline to come to the homestead to help with Zak while Bruce was away working at a gold mine. Much of Sue's attention had to be on gardening, the only way they could have fresh produce in the short growing season and canned vegetables in the colder months.

Sue was also working on the house they were building, a house with wood floors, unlike the earthen floors in the small cabin they'd built when they first started the homestead in 1974. A tent had been their home for seventy-seven days, while they'd built the one-room cabin[1], setting it against a small hill and using the hill as one of the walls, the ground as the floor, and sod for roofing. The new house would have ample space for a family with a growing child. But with Bruce at the gold mine and the nearest neighbor four miles away, Sue needed help with Zak.

Earline's route took her from Denver to Anchorage, where she spent the night. At seven the next morning, she boarded the quaint train that would take her to Fairbanks. A long delay because of a rockslide between Denali and Fairbanks had her arriving in Fairbanks at 9:30 that evening. It'd taken fourteen hours to go that 359 miles.

After a brief stay with Sue's aunt and uncle, Earline, Sue, and Zak headed up to the gold mine on Deadwood Creek, near Circle City to see Bruce. Here she was, out in the bush in Alaska, watching, being part of a gold-mining operation. All of it fascinated Earline. She kept a journal of some of her time in Alaska so she could share the experience with Peggy Scofield, the Miz Scofield of those early Colorado days; it proved to be the only time Earline would ever keep a journal. She'll later say it was the only time she had time to keep one. That the entries aren't daily gives a clue that she kept plenty busy.

≫•≪

[Undated]
Sure was good to see Bruce again. Sue, Zak, and I drove up in a rented truck—about 160 miles to the mining camp. We arrived late in the afternoon.

The camp was miserable: built on a pile of rocks; a small trailer with mining equipment strewn around; a tepee for sleeping. After the first night, I slept in the truck, which was more comfortable and had more mosquito control. Weather was not the best.

Gordon and Steve are awfully nice guys. Steve quite an imposing figure—played ball with the New York Giants. Gordon has a ranch in Idaho.

The guys at the mine are using a potato combine in their work.[n.b.: Gordon having brought his potato digger from his ranch in Idaho, tailored it to use for sluicing and classifying the rocks, which meant sorting out anything larger than two inches and dumping it.]

I was staying in camp with Zak while Bruce and Sue went out for a while. About 1:00 a.m. this huge man enters the tipi. I knew he was with the other guys, and they had come in. He didn't know that anyone was in the tent. Scared him. Got his gear and went out.

We stayed at the camp till Monday, then drove back to Fairbanks.

Chapter Twenty: North to Alaska

While [at the camp] Gordon gave Bruce the day off and we went to Circle City. Saw the Yukon River. Was a thrill to see the mighty Yukon.

That night we went to Circle Hot Springs for a bath and a swim. Had a drink in the saloon after.

On the morning we left the camp, Steve fixed a nice breakfast and served us—potatoes and eggs. And I washed the coffee pot!

❖

Seeing the gleaming pot sitting by the camp stove, Steve pointed at it, yelling out, "Oh no! You didn't wash that, did you?"

"Well, yes," Earline said.

"That'll ruin the coffee. We just got it seasoned right. Washing it messes everything up and we'll have to start all over again!"

Earline let them stew in their coffee thoughts for a few minutes, and just when she thought the guys were wrought up enough, keeping her voice calm and innocent, she said, "The outside is clean, but not the inside. I didn't wash that."

A collective sigh of relief sluiced the air.

❖

Then Gordon brought in the gold. It was shocking to see so much gold. The large nuggets were almost vulgar to look at! I thought the fine stuff prettier. Gordon gave me a nugget. I was thrilled. He let us take the gold outside to make pictures. He didn't even watch us.

They leave that gold lying around camp. Very interesting man that Gordon.

Zak said "MaMa" very clear while Bruce and I were talking at the truck. Zak was glad to see his DaDa.

We sure hated going away and leaving Bruce on that pile of rocks.

[While at the camp] Sue showed me how to pan gold. Too slow for me. Hurt my back and froze my hands. Only got a fleck in each pan. I would have to get fist size nuggets to do that.

It was daylight all night. Could read any time.

Steve had a dog team there. They were fierce looking dogs with white eyes. You don't pet sled dogs. I feel sorry for the dogs chained up all the time. I don't think I will ever watch dog sleds with a happy heart. I have a feeling inside that this Alaska makes people cold and cruel to animals. I don't think they really are or were to begin with, but become this way. I guess it is survival.

I don't understand why I feel a sadness of heart about this country. That is the strongest feeling I have had so far. It seems such a struggle to do anything, but it is more than that. I think I would name this heartbreak country—as well as backbreaking.

Earline, Sue and Zak went back to Fairbanks before heading out to the homestead in a little bush plane. Flying over one hundred twenty miles of tundra and scraggly black spruce forests of the Tanana Valley, the pilot landed the plane on a gentle hillside, using the landing strip cleared by Bruce and Sue soon after they arrived in '74. After unloading passengers and supplies, the pilot flew off again leaving the three Wilsons to their own devices.

The little one-room log cabin with its sod roof on the one hundred sixty-acre homestead tract would be Earline's home for a while. It was surrounded by soft hills, big meadows and forests, a creek from the Cosna River that ran by about sixty yards away.

Thursday, August 5, 1982

Today Sue and I picked berries, wild raspberries and currants. Sue made jam. Zak has a new tooth today.

Yesterday, August 4, we finished up the garden—weeding and hoeing. Sue has beets, cabbage, broccoli, garden peas, potatoes, a strawberry patch, lettuce and beans.

Today we had Mex. food for dinner. We have had moose-burgers, fresh garden salad several times. Stir-fry vegetables from the garden.

August 11

Well, today I really did it. My back went out and I yelled. Sue put

Chapter Twenty: North to Alaska

me to bed with a hot water bottle. The pain was bad for a while. Sue and Zak went to the new house to work. They have only been gone an hour, and it is so quiet it makes me nervous! Come back, Zak!

Sue is an excellent cook and we have great meals. Moose is the best meat I have ever tasted. We have fresh vegetables from the garden—nothing like those potatoes and peas. Quite often we have pancakes for breakfast, with fresh ground wheat flour. The grinder has not been working just right. Sue can't figure out just why.

It seems strange that you really can't tell one day from another—or stranger still when the day starts. It is getting dark for a couple hours now at night about 1 or 2 a.m. We are losing six to eight minutes each day of sunlight.

It has rained a lot since I came. A few days of sun and breeze. Everything is so green.

The new house is so nice—airy and light—sitting on a hillside. If the trees were thinned, you could have a view of the mountain range. I love the view of the mountains.

I must not forget Sue's root cellar. That is the ideal refrigerator! Under a trap door in the floor is a small dugout place. It keeps food colder than in most refrigerators. At least 40 degrees; I would say 38 degrees.

Oh lordy, I must get out of bed and go to the outhouse—uphill. Pray my back doesn't collapse on the trip! Nice outhouse. No door, but who needs a door? Certainly no one to see you. Company comes by airplane! And you can hear them before they get here. Two weeks here and I have seen only one other person—Dave, the owner and pilot of an airplane, several miles away. He delivered some groceries for us one day. He stopped one morning on his way out for a hunting trip, to check out the generator for our wash day! I did not see him that day, for he stopped on the landing strip some distance from the cabin. Generator was at the new house, about 2 miles uphill—1 mile down. [It was really about ½ mile!]

Wash Day, August 9

Sue brought the generator down and had to use it without a muffler. Took all day to do the wash on her Maytag wringer washer. She hauled the water up the day before on the weasel [a tractor-like machine] That weasel is some contraption.

Sue can do about anything there is to do around here. She is building windows for the new house.

August 10

We had word on Trapline Chatter from Betty Burg that Bruce had called her and said he had killed a black bear in the mining camp— and that Sue's $1,000 check was in from the State. [n.b.: Annual checks to Alaska citizens for oil rent dividends, began in 1982.]

August 11

We had stir fry vegetables and rice for dinner. Back is better today. I can walk around fairly well. No bending over tho.

August 12

This morning Sue picked raspberries off the [sod] roof of the cabin for our breakfast.

August 12

Frank Nyholm said on the radio this morning to Sue that he killed another bear yesterday. He had his generator running and was using his spray painter and felt something breathing in his ear, thinking Dave the pilot had landed and that it was Dave's dog. He turned his head and there was a bear panting in his ear! So he sprayed him with his paint sprayer, ran to get a 45 pistol he had, bear on his heels, and shot him saving one bullet for himself in case he hadn't killed him. Frank killed another bear a few days ago in his shed.

Dave dropped in about 4 p.m. Brought some fresh sheep meat, so with our potatoes and cauliflower, we will have sheep steak. He really seems to be a nice guy—but surely needs a bath!

After dinner—Man what good eating! Better than beef any day! The sheep in Alaska is the White Dall Sheep. A beautiful animal.

Chapter Twenty: North to Alaska

August 13

Tonight we had caribou for dinner. It is good meat. The meat that I have eaten here does not have a gamey taste. Dave brought it over yesterday with the sheep meat.

Rained all day! Sue bottled about 60 quarts of beer today.

August 14

Sue is making a Frostline jacket. To sew she must first organize, then get the generator going, and a light in the cabin, and machine in and connected up.

Sunday, Aug 15

Dave and Frank came over today. Had dinner. Dave brought fresh halibut that he had caught. It was great. Nice to have a visitor.

August 18

About 6 p.m. Dave flew in and the dog barked and carried on. Zak was having a fit over the plane buzzing the cabin. Sue ran up to the landing strip. We had mail—2 letters from P. Scofield, one from Paul, one from Wilbur. Sue and Bruce's checks came from the State of Alaska of $1,000 each. Package from Carol for Zak. [n.b.: Dave always circled the cabin to announce he was dropping the mail pouch. The pouch had a ribbon on it so it could be found more easily.]

August 21

We flew to Lake Minchumina today. It truly was a gorgeous day Just right temperature. The whole community was at the air strip—those friendly, wonderful people.

Mary Flood [n.b: an Alaska Native friend] took me out in the boat on the lake. Mt. McKinley snow capped from ground to lofty top. And fishing in that lake was the most exciting thing I have ever done—with the mountains shining above.

Saw a young moose walking in the water but couldn't get close because its mama would charge us. We saw three swans flying, and heard loons crying.

On my second cast I brought in a huge northern pike. He wouldn't fit in the net and finally lost him. I caught one other, about a two-pounder, on a red and silver spoon.

We rode to the boat on a three-wheel Honda with a cart behind. Mary and I rode in the cart. Out of film and couldn't get a picture of it.

The trip out was good. Zak was a sweetie. Came home, cleaned and cooked and ate the fish by 8 p.m.

August 30

Sandhill cranes flew over. I heard but didn't see as Zak was in high chair. Later saw some of them in trees.

≫•≪

BECAUSE THE CABIN CONSISTED OF ONE ROOM AND ONE BED other than Zak's, Sue slept on some blankets on the floor. Earline slept in the bed that she'd given them for a wedding gift years before. They'd managed to have it taken out to the homestead.

During the day, while his mother worked, Earline took care of Zak. She'd read to him, book after book, sitting side by side on the bed, the main piece of furniture in the cabin next to a table and chairs. Once she'd finished a story or a book, one-year-old Zak would comment, "Ahh-humm," and await the next.

Summer rolled on. Labor Day weekend arrived. The plan had been for Earline to leave as Sue's parents arrived to take over grandson duty. Dave flew over to pick up Earline for the trip into Fairbanks. On the way, they started to run out of gas, so they had to turn around and head to the nearest fueling place, which was Nenana, a tiny airport between the homestead and Fairbanks, sixty miles from Fairbanks.

Earline, having been away from banks for a while, had only forty dollars for the trip home. She gave Dave twenty. They arrived at the airport where Earline met Sue's mother and father, and she also saw Bruce for a short visit before boarding her flight. She hated to say goodbye to Bruce, but she did look forward to being home.

Changing planes in Anchorage, Earline, who had had no breakfast and thought she'd die of hunger, wanted to get a quick bite to take on the plane with her. She hurried into the coffee shop for a

Chapter Twenty: North to Alaska   199

roll and cup of coffee, and although that took little time, when she got to the gate, she saw her plane taking off. A sinking feeling in her stomach, she watched the plane rising from the ground and fly south.

She managed to get another flight to Seattle, but that was as far as she could go until the next day. She was stuck there overnight with only her twenty dollars plus some change left. She rued the day a couple of years back when she and Peggy Chavez had been at the beach and someone had taken off with their purses—credit cards and all. It had been such a hassle to cancel the cards that she'd never replaced them. Now she called around to find a place near the airport to stay the night and found one that cost twenty-two dollars, and it had shuttle service. She took it.

The next morning, Earline flew home on a non-stop flight to Denver. With her she had diamond willow branches for walking sticks and a set of moose antlers. Twenty plus years later those antlers would hang over the fireplace in Harry Sneads's home in Sneads. But the trip and all the adventure of Alaska would hang in Earline's memory forever.

1. They moved into the cabin on September 30th; three inches of snow fell on October 4th.

Chapter 21

The Greatest Heartbreak of All

In the late afternoon hours of May 1st, a phone call brought terrible news. Susan, in the hospital in Gillette, Wyoming, had undergone surgery to remove what the doctors believed was a benign tumor in her stomach. But it turned out not to be benign, and the cancer had spread. Susan, they said, had a year.

Earline, wild with worry, made a flight reservation, quickly packed a bag and left immediately for Gillette. She was there with her younger daughter at the end, just ten short and nightmarish days after the cancer's discovery. It was May 10, 1991. Susan had been just forty-one years old.

Stunned, disbelieving and desperate with grief, Earline and Bruce, who'd come down to Gillette from Fairbanks, journeyed on to Carol's home in Denver. Carol had been with her sister during the early days of tests and through the surgery, but an out-of-state commitment had required her to be away briefly for several days after they'd received Susan's wrenching prognosis. The plan had been for Carol to return to Gillette to nurse her sister through her post-surgery recovery but, instead, she flew back to Denver to join her mother and brother. There, the three of them grieved together, trying to absorb and make some sense of their sudden loss.

Three days later, family and friends gathered with Earline on a sunny mountainside to say goodbye to Susan and to honor her full but all-too-brief life. Although Earline knew her daughter was well respected and loved, the number and range of people who came to stand with her on that hillside, some who had traveled long distances, astonished her. Vance Gillette, Susan's former law partner and friend from North Dakota; Governor Lewis's daughter from New Mexico to represent her family and the Zuni Nation; Joe Athens, also from New Mexico; neighboring ranchers, friends from across Colorado, and many, many others came to say their goodbyes on that Monday in May. It was the day after Mother's Day.

≫•≪

STILLPOINT. SUSAN'S QUIET, LOVELY RESTING SPOT WAS THE place that, over the past few years, she had worked so hard to keep intact. Those beautiful one hundred sixty-six acres of land in Colorado's south-central Wet Mountains had been founded as an intentional community in 1978 by her friend Gia-fu Feng. Seven years later, upon his death in 1985, Gia-fu's share had come to Susan. She'd been his friend and Stillpoint's attorney, but she'd had no idea he intended to leave his portion of the land to her or his affairs in her hands. And there had been plenty of affairs to keep those competent hands of hers busy—grocery bags full of tax receipts, a community in shock, attachments to the land. Though it had been tough going, she'd managed through it all, even in spite of the minor car accident six months after Gia-fu's death and its repercussions that would go on to further complicate every aspect of her life. Because the State Farm Insurance Company refused her appropriate medical treatment in the wake of the accident, Susan's situation took a surreal turn, with scenes playing straight out of some dark work from the theatre of the absurd—she lost her law practice, her livelihood, and home; at the time of her death she'd been pressing a major lawsuit against the insurance company in federal court.

Through all this, her daughter had endured and kept moving forward, but now she was gone. Earline, beside herself with grief, knew this was one time it would take everything she had to go on.

Chapter Twenty-one: The Greatest Heartbreak of All Postcard Days

For Bruce and Carol, and in Susan's memory, she would go on.

Spending time in Colorado and Florida during the next few years, Earline, who was well-schooled in pushing through grief and sorrow, withstood the loss of her youngest child, her kindred spirit. Still, it was the greatest heartbreak imaginable.

Chapter Twenty-Two

Bearing Up

It was late spring, 1994. Earline had come to Stillpoint more than a month before and couldn't see herself leaving. The quiet, the stillness, this place Susan had so loved was just what she knew she needed to help calm the angst and agitation of the last three years. Those last few trying months in Florida had proved the tipping point. In the midst of the intensity of helping to care for her oldest brother Red, being with him in the hospital at all hours and in the presence of the awful human traffic there—the endless pain, the smell of antiseptics and hopelessness, his and others—she'd begun to long for the west again. A place of no cars, no bustle, no people was what she needed and wanted. And now, here, it was just Earline, the mountains, trees, and the creek. Without a doubt, this last month at Stillpoint had been the least stressful period of the past three years and was, very possibly, the most pleasant time she'd had in all her seventy years.

Earline knew she'd need to move forward again, but as yet she didn't know in which direction and, for the time being, she didn't much care. Summer at high altitude, in the tranquility of this blessed solitude, she was here, now, and she knew it for the respite she needed. Sinking down into the old sofa, breathing in the crisp evening air, she relaxed, clearing her mind, letting herself settle into being completely, utterly present in the rustic little cabin. Far removed as she was from everything except beauty and stillness, she at last felt herself beginning to heal.

A sound out on the back porch interrupted her musings, something unfamiliar. Someone tiptoeing across the porch? She thought she'd better have a look. There was no phone in the cabin, no police to call. There was no one else around, at least no one who was supposed to be there, which had been the appeal of course. But, she thought as she heaved herself up from the couch, all that great solitude also had its downside.

She crossed the short distance to the window; peering out, she saw nothing but solid black. No moon that night, and the stars weren't yet at their brightest. She moved on to the flimsy, glass-paned back door and edged it open just a little, enough for a peek.

Her heart caught as she found herself looking straight at an enormous, furry back, its owner's attention completely absorbed by the woodpile beside the porch. Furrowing and scratching through the wood, the bear was busy throwing large pieces aside as if they were matchsticks.

Through a surge of fear and astonishment, Earline tried to think what to do. It came to her as an image: the shotgun Bruce had given her last fall for her seventieth birthday, the wonderful Winchester Defender, 12-gauge, three-inch magnum shotgun with an eighteen-inch barrel—and a kick like a mule. And there it stood in a corner nearby. She'd fire it and scare that bear off.

With the shotgun in hand, she realized that only one of the windows near the bear opened, and it was a tough one to close. And so, if she didn't want to put a hole in a wall, the only thing to do was shoot out the back door—where the bear was, by the back door. Looking out again, she saw it had found the chicken bones she'd neglected to take down to the disposal area. Well, she thought, this had to be done, and summoned her courage.

Ever so gently, she pushed open the door, which in turn nudged the bear a little. The chicken bones held its attention, but it obliged

Chapter Twenty-Two: Bearing Up

by scooting forward a bit. Wasn't much of a scoot, but it was enough for her to poke the barrel through the small opening. She aimed high, not wanting to hit the bear or any other creatures that might be lurking around out there in the night, and squeezed the trigger. The shot rent the night air, startling the bear, which lurched backward on its haunches, hitting the door. The door then knocked the gun out of Earline's hands and into her shoulder, numbing it instantly, then clattered to the floor. Like the bear just before her, she staggered backwards. But seeing the barrel wedged in the open the door, she scrambled over, grabbed up the shotgun and pulled it toward her, watching with relief as the door swung shut.

By this time, the bear had lit off for the hills, but Earline knew there was every chance it could come back. She sat herself back on the sofa, again trying to calm down and think what to do. The battered old stake-body truck sat outside, but its lights didn't work and with no moon she wouldn't be able to see well enough to get down the rough trail and over the narrow bridge across Middle Hardscrabble Creek. Besides, she didn't particularly want to step outside and into the night, knowing the bear could be nearby.

The cabin had a little-used sleeping loft, but with the old ladder rotted, there was no way to get up there. Still, she could try. She dragged the chest-of-drawers over under the opening and climbed up on it, stretching all five foot, two inches of herself as high as she could. But she couldn't even reach the opening. She knew then there was little to do until daylight, when at least she might see if the bear was hanging around.

With the Winchester Defender across her lap at the ready and a watchful eye on that rickety back door, Earline spent a sleepless night there on the sofa. In fact, the bear did come back and did so, what seemed to her, every hour on the hour. Each time it nosed around, bumping against the door, and then ambled off, only to return again, like clockwork.

As soon as it was completely light, Earline ventured outside to look for wood to build a ladder. Though she had no saw, she did have a hammer, some nails and good reason to use them. Eventually, she found enough old wood scraps to suit her and, by late afternoon, she'd fashioned them into an odd-looking, but serviceable ladder, tall enough and stout enough. Pulling it inside, she propped it against the loft's opening, pumped up an inflatable mattress and moved her sleeping quarters up high.

That night, the bear sent her two cubs up to the cabin. Earline figured they'd smelled the chicken on their mama's breath and wanted in on the action. All through that second night of mostly sleepless, long, dark hours, the two youngsters knocked on and bumped against various doors and windows trying to get in.

After that, Earline stayed close to the cabin for several days, but eventually started to walk longer distances. She'd grown accustomed to the bears knocking on windows and doors at night, although it still unsettled her. She'd taken to closing the windows when she cooked, and she certainly didn't leave any chicken bones or other garbage outside. Even so, one morning, as Earline inched down the ladder, still half-asleep, she looked over to see one of the cubs standing with its paws on the windowpanes of the back door, peering in. As she jumped to get her camera, the abrupt motion startled the cub, which ran away from the cabin but stopped at the edge of the clearing. Although she didn't know where Mama Bear was, photo-loving Earline stepped out on the porch to shoot a picture of her morning caller.

She fashioned what she called her "late evening place," a quiet, fairly protected spot on the steps where she could lean back against cabin, where she felt safe, to watch the animal life around her. That's where she was sitting one evening when a cinnamon-colored bear lumbered right by her. A half-grown cub, he walked within twenty feet of her, not even glancing her way. That he either didn't see or care about her made her very happy.

Another late afternoon as she sat in her little spot enjoying her

Chapter Twenty-Two: Bearing Up

book, the gurgling stream made the only sound in the soft air. A flock of familiar wild turkeys wandered through the clearing, and later a fox ran by, intent on its destination. Then, through the branches and leaves, she thought she saw the tawny color of a deer. It looked bigger than a deer, though, so she thought maybe it was an elk. But it didn't seem big enough for an elk. Neither deer nor elk, it proved to be a cat, a very big cat.

The mountain lion had Earline in his sight as he sauntered to the old goat corral less than a hundred feet from where she sat. Effortlessly, it climbed up onto the top rail. The railing, about four feet high and made of scrub oak, was slender but strong, and it held steady as the lion stretched his muscular body and lay down along it, his eyes never once wavering from Earline.

Too frightened to move and too frightened not to, she wished she were in the house, and she wished she had her camera. Slowly, steadily, she stood up, slipped backwards through the door, and closed it behind her. Gulping for air and hearing her heart pound, she hunted up her camera and tried, from the safety of the cabin, to take a picture of the magnificent cat. Disappointed, she found the dusk light too low to make getting a picture possible.

For a better view, Earline climbed up to her loft to look out the window and down at the lion; she watched until it was too dark to see him. Throughout that night, she kept hearing strange whining noises that got her thinking something was circling the house. With no idea what sound a mountain lion made, she thought it might well be him out there, circling, trying to figure a way to get at her. And then it struck her that, just as easily as he'd climbed up the goat corral fence, the lion could climb the tree growing nestled up against the cabin and come right through the loft window. The thought scared the daylights out of her, but there was nowhere for her to go.

That mountain lion did it for Earline, prompting her out of her quiet, restorative retreat and back into the wider world. The next day, with images of bears downstairs and a lion in the sleeping loft, she packed up her clothes and headed out. She would return to Stillpoint after that, and often, but not alone—not until she'd acquired a dog.

EARLINE AND CAROL MET IN FLORENCE, A PLEASANT LITTLE town only fifteen miles northeast of Stillpoint, and the closest town to it with the amenities Earline wanted. They were looking at houses with the idea that Earline would move back to Colorado from Florida. Living in Florence, she'd be close to Stillpoint and a couple hours drive from Carol, who by then lived in Boulder. They'd looked at only one house when Earline said, "You know, I've always thought it would be fun to have a B & B."

As she talked about it, Earline's enthusiasm for the idea grew, sparking Carol's. Ultimately, mother and daughter found a charming little Victorian house on a corner in a quiet part of the quiet little town. It had a large parlor, kitchen and den, along with three rooms that could serve as guest rooms. Though the place needed work, it had obvious potential. Three days later, on August 29, 1994, they signed the contract. Earline had her next plan well in her sights.

She returned to Florida to pack up her belongings and move them to Florence. Earline was excited about her new project, one that called for creativity and held such promise. She was glad to once more have direction and specific purpose in her life, and although it would test her in many ways, she welcomed the challenge.

Chapter Twenty-Three

The Wilson House

EVEN AN EXCITING AND MUCH ANTICIPATED NEW DIRECtion has its tricky parts, and the first one for Earline came in packing the Florida house's contents into the big rental truck. That took four additional hard-working people. She enlisted the help of her long-time friend Rosa Lee Scott, who'd helped care for her children back in the 1940s and '50s, and Rosa Lee's daughter Claretha and a friend of hers who'd worked for a moving company. Rounding out the foursome was Rufus Burns, who, through the years along with his brother Roy, had often helped Earline with various big tasks. That day, the team worked hard and steadily and, at last, the house was empty and the truck full.

Next loomed the sixteen-hundred mile trip itself. Driving that big truck with her car on a trailer hitched behind, Earline would be making the trip from Florida to south-central Colorado by herself. Covering the long distance alone was no problem; she'd done that many times. The difficulty for her came in the unwieldiness of the rig—the backing up or turning around in a confined space with the car-trailer hitched onto it. The trailer jackknifed on her when she turned too sharply or tried to back up. But with little choice, she did what she always did in tough situations: she pressed on, trying to work through the situation. In this case, she looked for large parking lots in which she could turn around if necessary, but generally she tried to keep moving forward.

This move to Colorado was made in 1994, the same year Nelson Mandela visited the U.S., Lisa Marie Presley married Michael Jackson, and the U.S. economy was still making its way out of the 1990–'91 recession. Gas averaged $1.09 a gallon. This last was the most significant factor affecting Earline's trip, considering the load she was pulling. Other factors affected her along the way, too, and although they didn't figure into the general social context of the time, they did involve several incidents that would forever define that trip for her.

One was a traffic accident outside Montgomery, Alabama. Intending to head west, after a fork in the road, Earline had gotten herself on the wrong road. She needed to turn around, and needed a big wide area to do it. She eased the rig over to the median to wait for an oncoming SUV to pass. As she waited, like a bat out of hell, a car came speeding up behind her—on her left—hitting the side of her truck. The impact knocked her truck two feet to the right. She watched, dumbfounded, as what looked to her like a racecar then spun off across the road and smacked the SUV on the rear of the driver's side. The so-called racecar ended up in the ditch, fiberglass frame shattered to smithereens.

A state trooper arrived, and the involved parties—all of whom were over the age of seventy—were standing around as he surveyed the scene: the shattered car in the ditch, the SUV with a big dent and scraped paint, the moving truck and trailer sitting mostly in the median, but also on a bit of the main highway.

The racecar driver pulled the trooper aside; Earline didn't know what was said, but in the end the offending driver didn't even get a ticket. The event both unsettled and angered her—the accident itself was bad enough, but she also resented the breach of justice involved. What was more, she had to worry about the rain coming through that hole in the side of the truck and damaging her furniture. After a stop to get the truck repaired in Meridian, Mississippi, she was back

Chapter Twenty-Three: The Wilson House

on her way, but the episode left her feeling less secure and confident.

Later Earline would think that locking the keys in the truck just outside Marshall, a little west of the Louisiana/Texas line may have been the worst part of the trip. It was midnight, and it had been a long, long day on the road. She'd stopped at a gas station and filled up the tank. With the rain pouring down in buckets, her truck gassed and ready to go, she discovered she'd locked the keys inside. The attendant tried but couldn't help, so she ended up having to call a locksmith who eventually came and unlocked the truck. After that, exhausted and weary, she drove the short distance into Marshall, found a room, and called it a night.

The next day, having driven the one hundred fifty or so miles from Marshall to Dallas, Earline was on the I-20 loop around the city and hungry, when she found a fast-food place where she knew she could get a quick bite to eat. She pulled into the drive-through and, just in time, saw the sign signaling the seven-foot clearance and stopped. At that point, though, there was no backing up, and she certainly couldn't turn around. She called the truck company.

In a rare stroke of good luck, she learned that the company was nearby. They sent someone over to unhitch the trailer so she could turn the truck around. Then he turned the car trailer around and re-hitched it to the truck for her. She couldn't have been more grateful and was relieved to be on her way again. She was equally grateful that the man led her out of the maze of highways and got her headed to Colorado. It wasn't on the highway she preferred, but at least she was going in the right direction.[2]

This episode increased the wear and tear on Earline's nerves, and she was glad to have Dallas behind her. She drove the remaining 719 miles to Florence, with an overnight stay along the way, without incident. In a newspaper interview done almost a year later[3], Earline reminisced about her trip from Florida to Colorado. Talking about driving a big truck with a trailer hitched behind, she advised reporter Diane Graham, "Don't ever do that!" She meant it.

Happy to have arrived in one piece and glad that Carol was there to meet her, she arrived in Florence late in the evening on Wednesday, October 19, 1994. The harrowing trip behind her, Earline could now set her mind on the promising venture of transforming an 1895 Victorian house into *The Wilson House, A Cozy Bed & Breakfast.*

Over the next eight months, that transformation brought many people and more long-term friends into Earline's life, just the tonic she needed. Jane and Fred Gifford were among the first. Looking for help to unload the truck, Carol went to nearby Fox Drug to ask if anyone there knew of possibilities. Someone did, and thus Jane Fox-Gifford and husband Fred came into Earline's sphere. Freshly back from living in Alaska, the energetic and multi-skilled couple were just getting their feet replanted on Colorado ground and proved to be ongoing and versatile support. Their good help started with unloading that truck and continued through house painting and myriad other projects.

Equaling the town's friendliness, the talent to be found in that community of about thirty-five hundred amazed Earline. She met handyman Nelson DeCampos, learning right away that he was also a stained-glass artist. Several of his specially designed creations—windows and lampshades—would soon grace The Wilson House. He and wife Zuleika hailed from Brazil, and Nelson, a great joker, referred to himself as the original Brazilian nut. At those times, Zuleika's gentle forbearance was belied only by a slight rolling of her eyes.

Across the alley, Virginia and Pete Gherna lived right behind Earline. Pete, a retired miner, had a green thumb and, later on during the growing season, shared his garden's delights with his new neighbor. She especially appreciated getting his good tomatoes, which ripened before hers, and in turn shared back from her robust vegetable and watermelon patch. Earline often visited Virginia, who had trouble getting around and spent much of her time in the house. The two friends enjoyed their frequent chats over a cup of tea or

Chapter Twenty-Three: The Wilson House

coffee. On numerous Sundays, Earline took Pete and Virginia to lunch, an extra-special treat for those two stay-at-homes. Virginia told her that she'd never met anyone so nice.

Through her other friends, she met Barb and Hubert Martinez, a couple who would not only stay in touch with Earline over the years, but would become close friends with Carol and David—Carol's other half.

But much of this would be in the near future. In the early going, Earline and Carol learned they needed to apply for a special use permit to operate a B&B, a novelty for Florence. But novel or not, the venture required town approval.

To their surprise, the Wilsons found that the process included meeting with planning commission representatives; filling out and submitting a special-use permit application, which included proof of ownership, proposed hours of operation, and a floor plan of where guests would be; obtaining planning commission approval to proceed to a public hearing; attending a public hearing; and acquiring final approval. It seemed like a lot of red tape for such a small town, but the Wilsons were glad someone was taking notice.

Earline welcomed her family's help in the effort to get the B&B underway. While she was primarily concerned with refurbishing the house, a huge and overwhelming undertaking in itself, Carol took the lead on the paperwork. Carol spent as much time in Florence as she could, given her multi-layered and demanding work directing a large school-university partnership with its vast number of programs and national affiliation, serving as co-chair of the State Professional Standards Board, periodic teaching at the university, and consulting on an evaluation of the School District of Philadelphia. Earline knew of her daughter's wide-ranging commitments, making her even more appreciative of her daughter's support of and help with the project.

She also welcomed the times when David could join them in Florence. David's consulting work in leadership and civic engagement kept him on the road quite a bit, but he lent a hand at whatever needed to be done whenever he could.

Bruce, experienced in building, plumbing, and heating, helped with the refurbishing. Down from Alaska, he could stay only a few weeks because his heating expertise was in great demand up there thanks to the early-December arctic temperatures. But Earline found her son a great help and good moral support during his stay.

Thursday, December 15th was the date set for the formal planning commission meeting at which the special-use application was to be considered. Earline laughed at the response when Carol, seeking sympathy for them and their project, told a planning commission member that she was spending her fiftieth birthday in that meeting. "You're really lucky to spend it with us!" he said. Carol wasn't so sure about that, but she was happy to be there to help her mother.

The commission granted provisional approval and set the public hearing for the following Monday evening. Mother and daughter didn't know what kind of turnout there might be on that cold December evening, thinking their project wouldn't be of much interest to the community. But they were wrong. The large city hall meeting room was filled to overflowing by the time the hearing officially began. With all the chairs taken, several people stood leaning against the back wall.

The planning commission chair began by describing the Wilson House proposal, asking Earline and Carol to fill in with details on several points. When he invited members of the community to speak, the first person said how happy she was to have a B&B in the community. "When I have out-of-town guests, it isn't always possible for them to stay in my small house, so having this resource will be a great help."

Several more citizens spoke along this same line—Florence offered few places to stay, whether people were there on business or pleasure. And with the new prison, SuperMax, opened that year just outside town, there was a need for more options.

Then, the tone changed. A woman who lived about a block from

Earline's house stood up and walked to the front of the room. Her stiff posture and stern look gave Earline pause, and her words gave her reason to sit up even straighter.

"What about the parking?" the woman demanded. "We can't have cars cramming the area. And think of the undesirable people this'll bring in! We don't need that in this town." Then she glanced over at Earline and went on. "Who are these newcomers to start trouble in our town?"

Another person stood to agree, followed by a low rumble of voices that ran through the crowd.

Then a man wearing a dark blue feed cap stood up. Small and wiry, he moved from the middle of his row to the aisle, his slight body rigid with determination. He marched to the front of the room, turned to face the crowd, and in voice bursting with indignation thundered, "There's plenty of parking space! I live right behind Ms. Wilson, and I know what's there." He glared into the crowd. "And I also know what a good neighbor she is, and so is her daughter. These wimmin are good wimmin! And they're a good addition to this town. And all you sons of guns who don't think so, don't deserve to live here!"

Starting back down the aisle, he halted and looked squarely at the husband of the woman who'd spoken against the B&B. "You old bustard!" he sputtered.

Delighted laughter and applause followed Pete Gherna back to his chair. Someone else got up to support Pete's comments, and as the energy settled, the chair called the hearing to a close. The show was over.

It was only a few days before Earline and Carol learned the permit had won full approval. And then Earline really got to work.

"Biting off more than she could chew" came close to describing what Earline found in the refurbishing of that old house. As so often happens in renovation, one thing led to another, with the tearing out of old carpet, scraping of walls, updating of plumbing and electricity, building of cupboards, adding on an upstairs deck, laying a brick patio off the downstairs den; project after project presented itself in a seemingly endless feedback loop. And living in the midst of all the ongoing hubbub proved challenging, but she persevered.

June Lease, Earline's friend from the early 1960s when they'd lived in Golden, came down to Florence to help and provide moral support. The two of them would occasionally escape the chaos, going to nearby Stillpoint for fresh air and quiet or to Pueblo or Colorado Springs to shop for supplies.

One of those outings had a most special purpose: to choose and bring home an eight-week-old collie puppy. Thus Princess came into Earline's life and changed her into a dog-lover forever. That small bundle of fuzzy gold and white instantly won her way into Earline's heart. She also found her way into almost everything else. Nothing was safe from her exploring, enterprising nose and mouth—not clothing, magazines, and certainly not slippers. Shoelaces were always in danger. Playful, mischievous, and cuddly, little Princess was indescribably cute. She would grow into a beautiful dog, whom many would call Lassie, and who would be a wonderful, devoted companion for Earline over the next eleven years.

For now, that pup kept Earline and June entertained, especially when they were objects of her tomfoolery. But when Princess teased others, Earline was even more amused.

One hot day when Nelson was working hard at Earline's, building a small storage shed, he took a break. After taking off his cap, a special one someone had given him, Princess trotted up, grabbed his hat, and took off with it. Nelson fell for the bait, chasing the playful pup and yelling for her to drop his hat. When she was a good distance away, she stopped and waited, then when he got closer took off again, running 'round and 'round the tree in the yard. Then she pranced back and forth impishly, head and tail held high, the cap hanging from her mouth. This went on for some time, but eventually Nelson did get his cap back, miraculously undamaged. But

Chapter Twenty-Three: The Wilson House

he'd learned his lesson and after that always kept his cap on around Princess.

June of 1995 brought the eagerly awaited opening of The Wilson House. Guests responded enthusiastically to the comfortable, pleasant rooms and delicious breakfasts Earline prepared and served. In that same newspaper piece, reporter Diane Graham described Earline's B&B this way:

> [The] Wilson House is set in a home built in 1895. The comfortable, shady house... has three bedrooms, a shared bath, dining room, and sitting room.
>
> One of the bedrooms opens onto a cool cedar balcony full of flower boxes.
>
> The house is bright and clean. Fresh paint and flowered wallpaper brighten the walls. Light colored Berber carpet flows throughout the rooms and up the banistered stairs.
>
> The bathroom, more modern than those in many B&Bs, is stocked with items guests may have forgotten. Stained glass windows and light shades add color and interest to the high ceiling rooms...
>
> Guests at Wilson House are treated to a full breakfast of quiche, home made nut breads, a margarita glass filled with fruit and melon, juice, coffee, tea, and sometimes bagels and cream cheese.[4]

※•※

David's sister, Deanna Chrislip, designed Wilson House business cards, brochures and letterhead, while her husband, Brian Hale, created a beautiful carved wood Wilson House sign to hang out front.

Earline joined the local Chamber of Commerce, expanded her network, and devoted herself to making the B&B a friendly place to which customers would want to return. And in that, she succeeded, delighting in the fact that some people showed up on a regular basis throughout the warm summer months.

Among her first guests was a couple who'd asked to allow their little girl to stay. Given the limited facilities—just three guest rooms and a shared bath—Earline had thought it best not to permit children. But the couple persisted, and Earline relented. She was glad she did. Not only was the child no trouble, she was a delight. One morning the mother found her daughter and Earline in the backyard sitting on the marble bench under the big old tree. The little girl was shrieking with laughter as Princess darted over to her shoes, pulling exactly the right end of the lace to untie it. Each time, the little girl retied it, and Princess darted back over and pulled the lace again. Both girl and puppy seeming to enjoy it more every time, neither tired of the game. Such moments brought Earline great happiness; they left her feeling gratified and hopeful, even momentarily contented.

The winter of 1995–'96 proved a more challenging time. Florence saw few visitors during the colder months, and although Earline kept the business open, traffic was down. But that meant there was more time to spend with her friends, especially Zuleika, to mull over recipes, try out the delicacies Zuleika, a professional cook, produced, and share some of her own. Even so, Earline had lots of spare time and often felt at loose ends. She and Princess made frequent outings to Stillpoint, and she also occasionally drove up to Boulder to visit Carol and David, and they came down to Florence to see her. But by the time the warmer months approached, she was more than ready for the increased business.

Flowers blooming in profusion, her watermelons growing, herbs and tomatoes maturing, Earline tended her garden and flower boxes and enjoyed the results. Her guests loved the yard, as well as the house, and she went all out for them. Taking care of the nice people, providing a restful space and enticing food filled some need in her, that human desire to contribute in some way, to help others.

She worked hard, she worked steadily, and then Earline needed a break from it all. Spending the first couple of weeks in July visiting Bruce and Zak in Alaska seemed just the ticket. Carol would keep the B&B going and stay with Princess. By that time, Bruce and Sue had parted ways, and Bruce was living and guiding tourists at the Lake Minchumina lodge, on the same lake where Earline had fished

Chapter Twenty-Three: The Wilson House

with her Alaskan friend Mary thirteen years earlier.

Alaska held all the appeal of that 1982 trip. She'd also traveled up there after losing Susan in 1991, visiting Bruce at his cabin outside Nenana, a small community and historic Athabascan village situated at the juncture of the Tanana and Nenana Rivers. On all three trips, each occurring during summer months, she found the almost constant daylight disconcerting. But she knew she was glad not to be there in colder weather to experience the almost-endless night.

Bruce and Zak were glad to see her, and she them. She was also glad to see that expanse of lake water, the forests that framed much of it, and those regal mountains rising ever upward.

Although she enjoyed her time at Lake Minchumina, the feeling of being away from the rest of the world, isolated, brought her a sense of claustrophobia, of being fenced in. The trees seemed to close in on her, and she couldn't walk freely very far from the lodge, given the large grizzly bear population. After some time there and seeking more open and unrestricted movement, she flew back to Fairbanks, rented a car, and spent some time seeing other parts of Alaska.

First she stayed at a B&B in Fairbanks, which she enjoyed. Then she set off for Anchorage. There she found another B&B, and she also found a friend. Bridgette and her husband owned another B&B at Eagle's Nest, ten miles outside of Anchorage. Bridgette, stopping by on business at the place where Earline was staying, had struck up a conversation with her. The two ended up spending time together every day for several days while Earline was there. They'd go for fish and chips at a local hotel restaurant, and afterwards Bridgette would take Earline to see various sites around the area. They visited several museums—the Alaska Heritage Museum and the Alaska Museum of Natural History— among other spots.

Then that traveling gal headed to Seward. The road from Anchorage to Seward was a difficult one, with roadwork underway along parts of it. But after about a half-day drive, she finally arrived. There was such beauty in Seward, on the Kenai Peninsula and in the nearby Kenai Fjords National Park. The drama of steep mountains rising from the water, narrow inlets, all carved by glaciers, reminded Earline of pictures she'd seen in school geography books of the fjords in Norway. She loved water, and she loved mountains, and here the best of both lay majestically before her. She'd always remember these scenes, the panoramas of magnificent, breath-stopping splendor.

Once back in Florence, Earline had to face some increasing health concerns. She'd been having problems, and now her symptoms seemed to be increasing. She had heart palpitations and shortness of breath, and the doctor said her blood pressure was too high. Living at an altitude of 5,180 feet didn't help matters. Lower by 495 feet than Golden, where the family had moved from even higher Empire back in 1959 because of Bob's heart problems, the difference wasn't enough to be good for her condition.

It became clear that at almost seventy-three, she simply couldn't keep up the pace at which she'd been going. With her body and altitude conspiring to end her B&B venture, she recognized the obvious and realized it made sense to return to a lower altitude.

And so, in October, 1996, a little over two years after her arrival in Florence, Earline packed up again. Along with her beloved Princess and with their friend Nelson driving, she made the return trip to Sneads.

Ultimately, the house went on the market, and the next year it was sold. But the friends she'd made in that small town in those two years would remain in her life. Letters, phone calls, and Florida visits would span the miles and keep those friendships intact.

2. These events and other information about the B&B were chronicled by Linda G. Shelnutt in the July 11, 1996 edition of The Florence Citizen, "Forence's First Bed & Breakfast is 'Alive and Doing Well'", pp. 7 & 10.

3. "The Wilson House B&B Opens in Florence," *The Florence Citizen*, Diane Graham, Aug. 3, 1995, Vol. 98, No. 16, p.3.
4. Ibid, p. 3.

Chapter Twenty-Four

Matters of the Heart

Back in the days when Earline's daddy read adventure stories to his children, H. Travis owned the property on which Earline now lived. H. Travis's brother, known to everyone as Uncle Sim, owned an adjacent nine acres. The two brothers had been only the second title-holders of those two tracts, their owner and slave master having been the first.

Because Uncle Sim couldn't write, starting in the 1930s and continuing on through the '40s and into the '50s, Earline wrote his letters for him. Then, in the late 1940s as older men, Uncle Sim and H. Travis struck a deal with Earline and Bob. If the younger couple would take care of them, and then their wives after they passed on, Earline and Bob would have first rights to buying the land. And that's exactly how that land came to be owned by the Wilsons.

In the '50s, on what had been Uncle Sim's nine acres, Bob laid out the BruCaSue subdivision, using FHA financing to build the first houses sitting along the streets, three of which were named for his children. On what had been H. Travis' land, the smaller of the two parcels, Bob built his store in 1958. And behind the store, in 1965, he built the small house for himself, which Earline would later own and live in off and on for more than four decades.

Now, in 1996, after her two-year B&B venture in Colorado, she was back once more to her hometown in Florida. Over her years in that little house, she'd planted trees, shrubs, and flowers in its big yard, and now she got to enjoy all the mature, beautiful plants. And, of course, she took up where she'd left off, continuing to add to and refine the landscape. Amidst all that natural beauty, home again, Earline reconnected with family and friends and worked at creating an interesting and lively life for herself. Among those friends, she saw Pat and John Tenzer, a couple she'd met back in the 1970s when they ran the fishing lodge at Lake Seminole. She and Pat shared books, walks, recipes and plants. She also reunited with Dolly Seay and Margaret Pelt, whom she'd known and been close to since the 1940s. Her cousin, Essie, was another Earline loved spending time with. A while back, she'd rediscovered her cousin after fifty years of not knowing where she was. Now that she did, she didn't want to lose touch again. There was also Malba Lanier, a friend from childhood, who shared her love of fishing.

Malba and Earline would go off for a few hours or a whole day to try their fishing luck at various ponds, lakes and rivers in the area. One time in particular stands out in Earline's memory: their trip to St. George Island on the Gulf, 106 miles south of Sneads. Malba had a cozy retreat at nearby East Point, between Apalachicola and Tate's Hell State Forest, and the plan was to fish all day, then spend the night at Malba's. Traveling in separate cars, because Malba's little truck was filled with fishing gear and Earline had Princess along with her, they struck out. On the way down, they stopped at Whiskey Creek in Tate's Hell State Forest where they admired a beautiful lagoon, its waters deep, still, and mysterious. Tall lily-like grass adorned its shores. The woods surrounding it with its tall pines and dense palmetto bushes gave Earline an idea about why it was called Tate's Hell—she'd sure hate to be lost there, she'd said to Malba.

They headed on down to St. George Island, with its dazzling white sands and crystal clear blue waters, where they fished all day. They had no fishing luck at all, but they were lucky with their cameras, and took some wonderful photographs. Then, with daylight

Chapter Twenty-Four: Matters of the Heart

fading, the two pals piled back in their respective vehicles and headed for Malba's place.

Soon it was dark and, with the long line of cars and headlights streaming toward her in the oncoming lane, Earline missed the inconspicuous turnoff to Malba's. Given the heavy traffic, poor visibility and long way home, she decided to find a motel room.

The motel she found didn't allow pets, because, the manager explained to Earline, she thought they too often slept on the beds and that was unacceptable. Indignant at having her Princess accused of such improper behavior, Earline convinced the manager that Princess was exceptionally well trained and certainly never slept on a bed. Finally settled in their room for the night, the exhausted dog-owner took little time preparing for bed and soon was fast asleep. It was only when she awakened in the middle of the night and looked around for Princess that she saw her exceptionally well-behaved pooch stretched out, slumbering away—beside her on the bed.

AUGUST OF THE NEW MILLENNIUM BROUGHT AN ESCALATION in health problems for Earline. Learning that she had major blockages in several arteries, she followed her cardiologist's advice for the insertion of stents. On the phone with Carol two days after the procedure, she said she felt wonderful, never better. Her euphoric take on her condition made what happened the next day seem even more unbelievable, for on August 22, 2000, Earline suffered a severe heart attack.

The pain hit hard. It was excruciating. She couldn't get her breath. She could barely move. Somehow she managed to call 911.

An ambulance came and took her the twenty miles to the nearest hospital in Marianna, which proved inadequate for the severity of Earline's condition. Stabilizing her as best they could, the medics bundled her back into the ambulance and headed for Tallahassee Community Hospital. The sixty-mile trip a nightmare, she suffered through spasms of piercing pain, not only from the heart attack, but from her sensitive back bouncing on the ambulance's hard cot.

As soon as her sister Betty heard, she called Carol, who flew in from Colorado to be at her mother's side; David joined her soon after. Bruce, his wife Marty, and Zak came from Alaska. Betty, Linwood, Joanne, Jack, Lou, J.W., Willie Mae, Rubye and Toby, her husband, were all there as well. Earline would later learn that they'd been told it was highly unlikely she would ever leave the hospital, or the Intensive Care Unit for that matter. For days, it was touch-and-go.

Family and friends came to the hospital to lend their moral support, although few were allowed to be with her. Her Tallahassee second cousin Charles, Essie's son, and his wife, Candie, were regulars at the hospital; their daughters Erin and Amanda visited, too. They generously opened their home to Bruce, Marty, Zak, Carol, and David.

David's daughter, Kelly, drove over from Destin with her children, Chris, Paige, and Dylan, and Rubye's son Van came from Fort Walton Beach. Pat, John, and their daughters Jill and Janet came. Clearly, Earline had a caring following and sizeable crowd rooting for her.

Amazingly, against all odds, Earline overcame the greatest possible challenge—she survived. Despite losing a significant percentage of her heart's ability to function, she slowly regained the capability to breathe off the ventilator. And bit by bit, calling on that extra-strength will and determination that had gotten her through so much in life, two grueling weeks later she was transferred to a rehab center.

She hated being in the center, actively disliked having to do the exercises the therapists led her through, and despised the food. But mostly, Earline lamented the loss of her freedom, her utter dependence on others. Carol, who stayed nearby with Candie and Charles, spent the majority of her time with her mother, but often made the trip to Sneads to check on Princess, the two cats, and other matters at the house. Joanne's daily feeding of the pets was a tremendous help

Chapter Twenty-Four: Matters of the Heart

and great relief to both Earline and Carol, given the forty-five mile drive between hospital and home.

Much later on, when the crisis was far behind them, Carol revealed to Earline what the doctors and nurses at the rehab center had told her, that her mother would be able to go home at some point, but she would never again be able to live alone. Again Earline proved medical opinion wrong. After only a few months, she was indeed living alone, but with some changes in her life. She couldn't do everything she'd been accustomed to doing before, and especially not at her usual brisk tempo. She had to slow down, and she adjusted as best she could. It was hard because she'd never been one to pace herself, to look ahead and save her energy for particular tasks. She continued to overdo, then would run out of steam and have to rest. The slowing down was among her biggest challenges, ever.

Over the ensuing years, she had other health bumps in the road, which she always met and dealt with. One such was the pace-maker/defibrillator device she had implanted in 2006. This came at the recommendation of Dr. Joseph Baker, who'd been part of her original treatment team, and who became her primary cardiologist. Earline trusted Dr. Baker completely and was grateful for his continuing wise and kind attention. Another of those health bumps concerned her eyes, specifically macular degeneration in the right one.

When he spotted the problem, quick-thinking Dr. Thomas Lawrence, her ophthalmologist, immediately sent Earline to Tallahassee's Southern Vitreoretinal Associates. There they treated her, including her in a clinical trial for a new intervention using injections of Lucentis directly into the vitreous part of the eye. It proved so successful for her that WFSU, the local public radio affiliate, interviewed her for a story on the new treatment. In that interview, Earline described her miraculous recovery, saying, "I was completely blind in that eye." She went on to tell how, after the first treatment, "first thing, looking out my bedroom window, I could see a flutter of wings about thirty feet away. Next, I could see color . . . there were baby hummingbirds." She attributed such improvement to Dr. Charles Newell and his expert use of Lucentis. Several years later, she was glad he was still treating her when her left eye required attention.

≫•≪

No doubt about it, Earline's life had changed. Rather than taking to the road and traveling on a whim, she did more to create interest in her life closer to home. Her yard, with its flowers, trees, and shrubs had always been important and now took on new significance. By 2011 she could boast having more than twenty varieties of trees, including cedar, pine, fig, lemon, crepe myrtle, eucalyptus, oak, persimmon, and sweet olive. Most special to her was a tulip tree she'd had planted in Susan's memory. Other plantings included banana, hibiscus, hydrangea, holly and roses, not to mention the herbs and vegetables she grew. Her green thumb ensured lush, colorful and fragrant surroundings.

Princess and the two cats, Mama Kitty and Emmy, were her constant companions. Small, wiry and energetic, Mama Kitty had been a stray, and a pregnant one, when Earline took her in. When the kittens came, some she gave away, but she kept tiger Emmy, the one destined to become her watch-cat.

Late one day, in the latter part of the fall of 2000, Earline had stepped out the back door when she saw something that sent a chill down her spine. She shouted to Carol inside, "Call Linwood! Quick! There's a huge rattlesnake out here, and he's coiled to strike."

Earline heard Carol talking on the phone with Joanne, then call back out to her that Uncle Lin wasn't available. Carol then tried animal control, but they had no one to send right away. Then Earline saw her daughter move to the screen door and stand for a moment to take in the scene. The position of the snake, the cat and Earline made it tricky to go out that door.

Mother and daughter were watching Emmy with some worry. Her feline eyes were glued to that rattler, and with every muscle in her body taut, she was prepared to pounce if the snake moved toward

Chapter Twenty-Four: Matters of the Heart

her and Earline.

Quietly, Earline slipped to the nearby tool shed where she picked up a five-gallon pail and a shovel, then silently moved back toward the snake. Emmy, whose eyes and body hadn't shifted a millimeter, was between her and the snake. Earline, still moving quietly and slowly, intended to nudge Emmy out of the way and prodded the cat's back with the tip of the shovel. The unexpected touch startled Emmy and, defying gravity, her tensed muscles shot her skyward. There she levitated, seeming to hang those several feet above the ground, looking for all the world like a cartoon cat.

Emmy's giant leap broke the tension for Earline and Carol, who erupted with laughter. They laughed so hard, they could hardly stand. But the snake was still there, and it wasn't laughing.

The spell broken, Carol ran to the front door, out and around to the back yard, just in time to see the snake lying partially uncoiled on the cement landing. Earline had dropped the pail over it, but missed its head. The exposed head, she whammed with the shovel, and the snake was a threat no more. They were certain the watch-cat Emmy felt she'd done her job.

≫•≪

It was after Zak came to stay for a while in 2001 that tiny black-and-white Molly showed up, looking for a handout and some shelter. Skin, bones and ratty fur, with a mean hiss, the young cat had obviously been living rough. Then not long after Molly's arrival, weeks-old Benjamin turned up. Earline and Zak had to trap him in order to feed and shelter him. Tough-girl-turned-sweetheart Molly took the kitten under her care and taught him the ropes. Emmy and Mama Kitty, having been in residence several years, felt the intrusion of the interlopers into their territory, but over time, the four fashioned for themselves a fairly peaceful co-existence.

Earline's pets were so dear to her that when, in the fall of 2006, she lost Princess to some unnamed illness, she was devastated. And this sad event coming right after getting the pacemaker, made it an especially difficult for her health.

Though she still had her four feline companions, still, after eleven years with Princess, life without a dog seemed far too quiet and lonely. Then in March of 2007, Earline's niece, Rubye's oldest daughter, Debbie, sent Earline an eight-week old ball of frenetic energy, and life got a lot livelier again. An Australian Shepherd, Josie came via Rubye and Toby, who'd driven hundreds of miles to meet Debbie half-way in the puppy relay. Earline had named the little one in honor of her late friend, Josephine Harris, Dr. Jo.

Within a year, to keep Josie company and help run off some of her boundless energy, Earline took in Penny, a young Chihuahua-Beagle mix. The four cats added to the two dogs kept Earline entertained, and they certainly kept her busy. But as much companionship as her pets surely offered, it still didn't quite fill the need she felt for company, human company. Though she'd lived in Sneads off and on all her life, she felt an increasing need for a stronger sense of community.

As a child, an older friend had taken Earline to the Sneads First United Methodist Church. She'd liked that and so, off and on over the years, she'd attended services there, and, in their younger years, had taken her children there for church and Sunday school as well. Now she was drawn to the kind and welcoming members and looked forward to occasions to be with them. But, still, it was a big step when, on October 24, 2010, after some eighty years of variable attendance, and with the encouragement of the new minister, Steve McCoy, Earline formally joined the church. Colorado friend Diane Thornton commented on the decision-making process, "It's nice to ponder your decisions before leaping in wholeheartedly."

YEARS BEFORE, IN 1993, EARLINE HAD URGED CAROL TO WRITE a biography of Gia-fu Feng, the man who'd left Stillpoint in Susan's hands after his death. At the end of Susan's life, she and friend Clara Reida had been editing Gia-fu's partial autobiographical manuscript. Later, it was Earline's opinion that Carol could take up the project.

Chapter Twenty-Four: Matters of the Heart

Having no background in Chinese history and philosophy and too much work in her professional life, Carol initially resisted the idea. But then, after the complicated legal matters of Susan's and Gia-fu's estates were settled, she decided to take it on.

Because of the multiple competing demands on her time, Carol had been able to work on the book only intermittently over the years, but then, in 2008, the book's completion was in sight. Mother and daughter sat on Earline's recently glassed-in back porch, soaking up the warm spring sun and talking about the forthcoming book. Their conversation meandered to some of Earline's adventures in Wyoming, in particular the incident with Annie Long Hair and driving across the frozen Wyoming and Montana landscape late at night.

Earline enjoyed recounting that tale, and her daughter loved hearing it. But she was more than surprised when Carol stared at her, with a smile and a twinkle in her eyes. "Mom," she said, "I should write a book about you!"

Then it was Earline's turn to resist, but over time the idea grew on her, just as the idea of writing Gia-fu Feng's biography had grown on Carol. And so they began, daughter interviewing, mother remembering, talking. Their conversations were recorded and then transcribed by Carol, who then turned it all into a book, about Earline. And now she'd sent the last draft, which Earline had promised to review.

Marty Smoker, friend and helper, had just left after taking the delighted Josie and Penny for a vigorous walk. The two dogs lay sound asleep on the floor, and Molly dozed on a chair nearby as Earline stretched out on the love seat where she liked to relax, the sun soaking her neck and shoulders. Emmy curled up at her feet and Benjamin leapt up to lie across her lap. The house quiet, the critters napping, Earline read the pages before her.

Memories can lie dormant; sometimes they sleep through time. In the course of thinking about the book, Earline had awakened many memories that had been sleeping for years. She knew some still were. There were remnants and reminders, like a 1940s photo of her with some Marines at a train station. She'd been surprised when Carol and Rubye had come across it and identified her as the sole woman in it, but she didn't remember who'd taken the photo, or even the circumstances of where it'd been taken or why.

Other photos, sometimes words or smells, triggered almost total recall of situations, people, places. Those memories purred in her mind, like Benjamin, lying there on her lap purring with such vigor. She could remember vivid details of her mother creating those tea parties for just the two of them, of her daddy reading adventure tales to his children, of her own travels and adventures with the carnival and across the country. She wondered what other memories might yet be sleeping; even through all the reviewing and reflecting of the past couple of years, she wondered what memories were yet to awaken. It was good to remember the past, the friends, family and places so important to her. And it also felt good to relax in this moment, with her companionable pets surrounding her, sunbeams saturating her very being. Scratching Benjamin under his chin, she listened as his purring filled the room, and she felt it fill her heart. She read on.

Acknowledgements

When I was thinking about how to thank the many friends and family members who helped bring this book into being, the image of nineteen-year-old Earline's cross-country hitch-hiking trip came to mind. Creating this book was, indeed, a trip in itself, a journey into the seemingly familiar, but much more vast territory of my mother's life than I could have known. It was a passage into the life of a person who is not only my mother, but a separate being whom I wanted to know better, and from a different angle, through another lens.

A lengthy expedition, this one, filled with starting points, good rides, long waits, open roads, back roads, dead-ends, wrong turns, comfortable cars, bumpy trucks, a sense of direction, or a lack thereof—you get the picture. Hitchhiking is not for the timid. Nor is writing a book about one's mother. Luckily for me, as it was for Earline some seventy years ago, generous people were willing to give me lifts, point me in appropriate directions, save me from really wide-of-the-mark turns, comfort me when I made them anyway, and provide nourishment when needed.

My mother, Earline, was the primary vehicle into this excursion. After some initial resistance to the idea of a book, she jumped in, willing to help navigate, as well as go along for the ride. She allowed me to interview her, then converse about, poke around in, and cogitate on what she shared. It would be difficult for any book to provide a complete picture of someone's life. My aim in this one was to honor my mother by relating stories of her life, the often difficult circumstances she's faced, the sometimes humorous and outrageous responses she's had, the courageous and determined spirit in which she's done it all. And all with her support, which she has generously given.

My brother, Bruce, when not short-sheeting my bed on common

visits to our mother or leaving me inventive gifts, like, say, pickled pigs' lips, has been tremendously helpful. His memory, much better than mine, filled in some big holes and helped me avoid likely detours. Besides being a delightful travel companion, he is a wise, kind soul, despite, or perhaps because of, his mischievous tendencies. The secret is, as wife Marty Wilson knows, he's quite tender-hearted.

As for family, my wonderful aunts and uncles responded to questions, provided photographs, and listened to my suppositions along the way. Thank you Rubye, Uncle Lin, Aunt Joanne, Aunt Lou, Aunt Willie Mae, Aunt Mary Alice and Uncle Jack. (Aunt Betty, Uncle J., Uncle Red, Melvin, and Jimmy, we miss you.) Shari, Rick, and Kim Messmer also lovingly gave their memories and encouragement.

Having a trip in mind is one thing. Having a map of the country another. Knowing how to make sense of it, what direction to go is yet another. Laura Goodman, editor extraordinaire, helped me find my way, suggesting alternatives, supporting me in my decision about a route that seemed feasible for my purposes, and guiding me along it. Through many afternoon strolls with precious pooch Macy, sit-down confabs over chapter draft after draft, she's been there with unflagging professionalism and wisdom, as well as kindness and good humor. She's the best editor in the world.

Looking back informs going forward. Before this book, I knew very little about the generation before my mother. My maternal and paternal grandparents had all passed before my parents even met. Bits and pieces of family lore survived, but little concrete data presented itself. Long-time (high-school buddy and college roommate) friend Delilah Blount applied her genealogy-research know-how and uncovered some initial family history. Candie Garner delved deeply into records of all kinds, coming up with my maternal family tree that extends back a couple of centuries. She is persistent, generous, and amazing. And she's married to my second cousin, Charles.

How to thank all those who gave me lifts in the form of feedback and encouragement in continuing down the road? Reading an early draft, Gary Holthaus suggested a different starting point. He was right, as usual. Rachel Weaver and Janelle Lyn made suggestions for creating more vivid scenes—along with other good advice; Mildred Chrislip, Jan Kerrigan, Harriet Simons, Jayne Satter read drafts along the way and pointed out some bumps to avoid. Charmaine Getz, writer of the unusual and carny buff, shared information and insights about carnivals of the 1940s and Electra's role in them. Homer Hirt steered me clear of problems about the Jim Woodruff Dam and Apalachee Correctional Institute.

Ongoing encouragement came from Clara Reida, Celia Barnes, Ellen Price, Carmen Baehr, Peggy Raines, Margaret Hatcher, Ann Foster, Barb Scheibel, Jaye and John Zola (and special thanks to John for publication guidance), Barb and Hubert Martinez, Kelly O'Shea, Marty Smoker, Pat Tenzer and June Lease. Also appreciation to my sister of the panhandle, Mona Bailey, who, as Earline overcame many health obstacles, dubbed her our Miracle Mom. What would I do without my friends?

Proofreading pals are my friend of five decades, Lois Kellenbenz, Suzanne Wilson, and conferring reader Sandy Schnitzer. You have my enduring gratitude, along with a lot of chocolate.

My destination was in sight when a lane closure sign appeared. Through the networking magic of Boulder Media Women (thank you, Carol Grever), exceptional graphic designer Sue Campbell came to the rescue. She brought her impressive talents to open the way and ensure that *About Earline* continued forward—and in style.

With me, as always, on smooth rides and along dark, troublesome back roads, is David Chrislip, truly my other half. I'm so grateful—and so glad.

The length of this piece reflects how many people contributed to the venture, and there are others not even named. My thanks to you all. I think we've arrived.

—CAROL ANN WILSON
Boulder, Colorado, February 20, 20011

About the Author

After almost forty years as an educator—teacher, high school principal, assistant superintendent, university instructor/visiting professor, school-university partnership director, and consultant—Carol Ann Wilson has now turned her full attention to writing. While in education, she published numerous journal articles and book chapters. Her favored genre now is creative non-fiction. Her first book, *Still Point of the Turning World: The Life of Gia-fu Feng*, won *ForeWord Review*'s Book of the Year Award for biography and was a finalist the Indie 2010 New Generation Award in nonfiction. She lives in Colorado, where her mother first took her and her siblings some fifty-eight years ago.

For more information: www.carolannwilson.info

Made in the USA
Charleston, SC
11 April 2011